CONTENTS

STUDY GUIDE

FOR

MUSIC LISTENING TODAY

Fourth Edition

Charles Hoffer, Ph.D.
University of Florida

Mary Ray Hoffer, Ph.D.
Santa Fe College

For product information and technology assistance, contact us at
Cengage Learning Customer & Sales Support,
1-800-354-9706

For permission to use material from this text or product, submit all requests online at **www.cengage.com/permissions**
Further permissions questions can be emailed to
permissionrequest@cengage.com

ISBN-13: 978-0-495-57201-5
ISBN-10: 0-495-57201-2

Wadsworth
25 Thomson Place
Boston, MA 02210
USA

Cengage Learning is a leading provider of customized learning solutions with office locations around the globe, including Singapore, the United Kingdom, Australia, Mexico, Brazil, and Japan. Locate your local office at: **www.cengage.com/international**

Cengage Learning products are represented in Canada by Nelson Education, Ltd.

To learn more about Brooks/Cole, visit **www.cengage.com/wadsworth**

Purchase any of our products at your local college store or at our preferred online store **www.ichapters.com**

Printed in the United States of America
1 2 3 4 5 6 7 12 11 10 09

Part V -- Romantic Music   97

Part VIII -- Music Around the World — **163**

Flash Cards of Musical Terms — **175**

PREFACE

This Study Guide is designed to help you get the most out of your music appreciation course and its text, *Music Listening Today,* fourth edition. It does this in several ways.

1. It can help you review the information in each chapter by

- Briefly listing the main points of the chapter, as well as offering several overviews of style periods

- Listing musical terms as they are introduced

- Providing flash cards of musical terms for review

- Concluding each of the book's eight parts with a brief listing of the notable features of that part or style of music

- Providing discussion and critical thinking topics at the end of each part

- Providing crossword puzzles as a review of terminology

2. It can help you gain greater skill in listening to music by

- Including three exercises that ask you to compare the musical features of works from different style periods

- Presenting a simplified listeners' score of the first movement of Mozart's Symphony No. 40 to help you follow what happens in the music as you listen to the work

- Providing links to two listeners' scores that can be downloaded to help you perceive what happens in the music

- Including a section on attending concerts

3. It can help you earn a better grade in the course by

- Increasing your success in connecting the information you learn with your ability to listen to music, which means that you will do better on examinations

- Providing suggestions for writing concert reports

- Offering review questions, practice terminology quizzes, and crossword puzzles at appropriate places. The answers to the questions and the solutions to the crossword puzzles are shown at the conclusion of each part.

Because many students today take music appreciation in online or distance learning courses, a section containing suggestions for students in nontraditional courses has also been included in this Study Guide.

Our wish for you is that you enjoy and understand music much more than you did before you took this course.

Charles Hoffer, Ph.D.
University of Florida
Gainesville, Florida

Mary Ray Hoffer, Ph.D.
Santa Fe College
Gainesville, Florida

GETTING STARTED

TAKING ADVANTAGE OF THE ACTIVE LISTENING GUIDES

Listening is a crucial aspect of learning in a music appreciation course. The two CDs enclosed with the textbook provide a "core" program of representative works, and the ancillary four-CD set contains all the rest of the works featured in the book. You can listen to these CDs on any CD player or on your computer.

Playback Equipment

The computer offers you several very helpful features. Your enjoyment of music, especially the music covered in this course, will be greatly increased by the use of quality playback equipment. It is strongly recommended that you avoid listening using only the speakers on a lap top computer. They are not designed for music listening, and many of the features in the music will be scarcely audible on them. If you have only a lap top, use either plug-in quality ear phones or attach quality speakers when listening to music.

Active Listening Guides

One of the benefits of listening on the computer is the Active Listening Guides that can be downloaded. These downloads will play on any Windows or Macintosh CD-ROM player. To take advantage of this feature, your computer must meet the following requirements

PC
- Windows XP and Vista
- Pentium II, 64 MB RAM
- 800 X 600, 16-bit color display
- 16-bit sound card
- Speakers or headphones
- 4x CD-ROM

Mac
• MAC OS 10.3.9 or later
• PowerPC Processor or later
• 64MB RAM
• 800 X 600, 16-bit color display
• 16-bit sound card
• Speakers or headphones
• 4x CD-ROM

Accessing the Resource Center and Companion Site

To access the Resource Center, go to http://academic.cengage.com/login and register your access code. This code is provided on the printed card that comes as part of a package with your new copy of the text. Otherwise, you can purchase an instant access code online from http://www.ichapters.com.

To download the Active Listening Guides to your computer, go to the Resource Center and click on the link as directed. Some of the additional resources at this site include lectures, interactive demonstrations of musical elements, and demonstrations of instruments of the orchestra. To download one of the files, click on the download icon and save it to your hard drive. If you have trouble downloading or operating the program, check minimum system requirements or the online User's Guide. You may also contact 1-800-423-0563 for assistance or go to www.cengge.com/support.

To access the companion site for *Music Listening Today, Fourth Edition,* go to www.cengage.com/music/hoffer/mlt4e. Here you will find links for the Internet Library, Listening Items for Tests, Chapter Quizzes, Powerpoint Presentations, and a demo plus four Active Listening Guides.

Studying with the Active Listening Guides

1. Insert the appropriate *Music Listening Today* CD in your CD-ROM drive.

2. Locate the folder for the Active Listening Guides that you have downloaded to your computer's hard drive and double-click to open it.

3. The Active Listening Guides will load and the title screen will appear.

4. To continue, click the **Contents** button at the bottom of the screen.

5. The Table of Contents screen allows you to navigate through the Active Listening Guides by clicking on the selection you would like to listen to and view. You can return to the Table of Contents screen at any time by clicking the **Contents** button that appears on every screen.

6. Click on the title of the work you wish to hear. A graphic representation of the work will appear as a series of colored umbrellas or sections on a bar.

7. A row of buttons can be seen at the bottom of the screen:

   Play arrow   Click to start or repeat the selection. As the selection plays, a triangle moves from left to right just below the line in perfect synchronization with the music. When appropriate, lines of describing the music, texts and translations of vocal works, and short music examples pop up on the screen.

   Double bar   Click to pause the music.

8. You will also see the following features for the works:

   Umbrella or section of bar   Click inside the shape, or move the vertical arrow into position, to play a portion of the work.

   Umbrellas or sections of the same color   Click to compare portions of a work.

   Commentary   Click to read information about the work and its context.

   Biography   Click to read a biographical sketch of the composer.

   Cultural setting   Click this occasional button to learn about a folk or world music selection.

   Contents   Click to return to the list of works on the selected CD.

   Glossary   Click to view definitions of musical terms.

   Internet Library   If you have an Internet connection, click to go directly to the Cengage Companion Web Site for *Music Listening Today, Fourth Edition*. Here you will find an extensive list of relevant web sites arranged under various topics. The sites are updated periodically.

   Listening Quizzes   The "Listening Quiz" button at the bottom of the screen offers a practice listening quiz on that particular work. The quiz's five to ten questions are intended to help you improve your listening skill. For that reason, they are <u>not</u> scored, and a question may be repeated as often as you wish. These quizzes, and especially the additional "Review Quizzes" that cover each CD, are very useful when studying for listening questions on examinations. When you click on the "Listening Quizzes" button, the first question will appear on the screen.

- Click on the CD symbol to hear the short segment of music. To hear it again, click on the symbol.
- Click the button next to your answer and find out if your answer was correct. If not, try again. Be sure that you can hear what makes the correct answer the right one.
- Use the forward or back arrow to move to the next or previous screen
- When finished, click on **Return to Listening Guide** or on **Contents** to return to the main index of the selected CD.

9. Click on **Quit** at the upper right of the screen to exit the program.

To Students in Nontraditional Learning Situations

For hundreds of years college classes have consisted of a professor and students meeting together in the same classroom or lecture hall. But that situation has changed for many of you today. Now you may never meet with an instructor, or see your instructor only once or twice with the remaining contacts by computer, telephone, e-mail, fax, or individually arranged conferences. Sometimes the instructor is seen only on a television monitor. If the situation involves closed-circuit television, class interaction may be possible; in other cases, it is not.

Although these situations vary quite a bit, they have one point in common: *students must assume much more personal responsibility than is needed in a traditional classroom setting*. This type of learning requires self-motivation, good time management, and the ability to work independently. Here are some suggestions for doing well in nontraditional settings.

1. Carefully read and follow the course syllabus, web postings, and everything you receive regarding the mechanics of the course. These materials contain essential information about matters such as when papers are due, when and how examinations are administered, and when and how to communicate with the instructor. Ignoring this information is the academic equivalent of driving your car around town with your eyes shut!

2. Follow the course outline! It lets you know what material will be covered and when something is due. Prepare a schedule for yourself when a chapter is to be read, a paper completed, or an examination taken. You have heard it hundreds of times, and it's true: *Do not wait until the last couple of weeks to complete your work for the course!* Cramming does not work well in most courses; in music appreciation it borders on being just plain dumb. There is definitely too much to absorb in terms of perceiving different types of music, to say nothing about the huge amount of information!

3. Read Point 2 again -- it's that important! It has been our experience that students in nontraditional learning situations either do the work and earn a good grade, or they don't, and the instructor must give them a low or failing grade. Please don't let that happen to you!

4. Set aside specific times to do your work for the course. If you wait until you're not busy, you probably will never get to it. Be sure to arrange for times to listen to the music on your CDs as well. Play them mostly on your computer so you can use the Active Listening Guides. Everyone - even students in traditional situations - needs to listen to the music outside of class if they want to do well. Those in nontraditional settings must rely entirely on themselves to do the necessary listening.

5. You *must* purchase the four additional CDs for *Music Listening Today*. Although this involves an extra expense, they are *absolutely essential* to compensate for the fact that you are not participating in a structured class. They are strongly recommended even for students who are in traditional situations. The CDs provide a tremendous aid in listening to the music. As you play one of the CDs that come with the book, an arrow follows the design of the work, letting you know exactly what is sounding at that moment. Additional information and reference points also show up on the screen. The disk is usable in either Windows or Mac forms.

6. Take advantage of the material in this Study Guide. For the reasons mentioned in its Preface, we believe it will be an invaluable aid to you!

7. If possible, talk to someone about what you are learning in the course. This person doesn't necessarily need to be taking the course. Verbalizing can help you learn as well as make the material more alive and relevant.

8. Try to get your family and friends interested in attending concerts with you. This not only makes if more enjoyable, but often others can provide helpful feedback on what you heard.

There are many advantages to taking a course in a nontraditional setting. Your choice in taking an online or web assisted music appreciation course, or one in another nontraditional setting probably indicates that you have self-motivation, good time management skills, and the ability to work independently. These are all admirable qualities!

But keep in mind that this type of course may be somewhat more difficult than one in which you meet regularly each week, because you do not have the specific demands of a regular class. As a general rule, a traditional three-hour course requires three hours each week in class and more than double that amount of time studying. So you should plan to spend a minimum of eight hours each week reading, studying, listening to your course CDs, preparing for exams, and doing whatever assignments are required by your instructor.

Although you will study more independently, your textbook and its related ancillaries are invaluable tools to help you along the way. *Music Listening Today* is very user friendly and is written in a style that is easy to understand, even if you have little or no previous training in music. The downloadable program for use with the CDs allows you to hear the features of works as they would be explained and presented in class.

Probably the biggest temptation for students enrolled in a course that doesn't meet regularly each week is to sit back, relax, and let things just sort of take care of themselves. The thought is that if nothing bad is happening, then everything must be OK. But the reality is, if nothing is happening, then nothing's OK!

Have you ever heard the saying "Never bite off more than you chew"? If you put off studying, listening to your CDs, and doing your assignments until deadlines approach, you will have to hurry and probably "bite off more than you can chew." So it might help to think of this: Compare digesting the information in the course to the way you should eat – a little bit at a time!

Attending Performances

Why do people go to a performance of music when they could listen to a recording of the same music at home with their shoes off?

Why Go to Performances of Music?

1. A sense of involvement is one good reason for going to a performance of music; it becomes a more real experience. As remarkable as recordings are, there is something about actually being present at a performance that cannot be duplicated in a recording. It's like being present at a theater production compared to watching a DVD of the performance. Because the DVD is not a live experience, the viewer is not as caught up in the drama.

2. At a performance the listeners gain a visual impression of the musicians, which adds to the total impact of the event. Seeing is particularly important in operas and musicals, because they are a type of drama. Even in the case of instrumental music the performers contribute to the effect of the music through actions involved in playing their instruments.

3. In addition, live performances are live. There is a freshness and vitality with each one. It's a happening.

4. Live performances often have the advantage of presenting music without the distortion that usually accompanies electronic amplification or the production of recordings. Some alteration of the real sound is routinely done in recordings of popular music. Furthermore, there is some loss between the actual sounds and their reproduction. It is difficult to compress the sounds of an orchestra spread across a 50-foot stage into a few speakers.

But attending a live performance is not always superior to listening to a recording. For example, you might have a seat that does not allow you to see very well, or you may sit near someone who causes distractions such as talking or shuffling a program while the music is being played.

What Kinds of Performances Are There?

There are many different types of performances, and each one differs in the kind of music performed.

Performances of art music are called concerts or recitals. The main difference between them is the number of performers involved, which affects the type of music performed.

- Recitals are usually for two to five performers and last about one hour to an hour and a half. Concerts are for large ensembles such as bands, orchestras, and choral groups. They are often a bit longer than recitals.

- A song recital is often for one singer with piano. Songs are generally shorter than instrumental works, therefore more titles are performed in the course of a song recital. Art songs are often in languages such as German, French, and Italian, and translations are sometimes not provided in the printed program.

- Both concerts and recitals tend to be somewhat more formal than other musical performances. The performers usually wear conservative clothing, so as not to detract from the music. There are no actions besides those directly involved with performing the music.

An opera is different. Operas are usually longer than instrumental concerts. They have scenery, acting, and costumes, as well as vocal and instrumental music. Operas are usually sung in Italian, German, or French, and less often in English. A program is provided that contains a synopsis of the plot. Often English translations appear on a screen above the stage. Sometimes a small book containing translations of the text (libretto) may be available. This is useful if the lights are not turned down so much that reading it is impossible.

Performances of popular music depend very much on the particular setting, which can range anywhere from very small auditoriums to huge stadiums. Performers wear anything from ragged jeans to brightly colored costumes. The visual element is very important. Almost all performances of popular music are miked. The audience often participates by clapping and sometimes singing along.

What about Conduct at a Performance?

Whether listening to a recording at home or sitting in the audience of a concert hall, the main point is to listen carefully and attentively to the sounds of the music and how they have been organized.

Distractions

Simply put, there should not be any at all. Concertgoers shouldn't talk, unwrap candy, shuffle programs, or be the cause of any distraction!

Applause

For instrumental works such as string quartets and symphonies and choral works such as oratorios, *never applaud between the movements or sections of the work!* Save all applause until the work is completed. It's not the same for stage works such as operas and musicals. Audiences applaud after important solos, duets, and choruses, and the applause can be spiked with cheers of "Bravo" ("*Brah*-voh" for males, "Brava" for females, or "Bravi, which is pronounced "Brav-vee" for mixed groups of performers), if the performers have done unusually well. In musicals composers often write a reprise ("re-*preeze*"), which is a repeat of the portion of the music just heard. This is done in response to the expected applause. Frequently after the conclusion of a program the performers will return to do an encore ("*on*-core"). Encores are short extra numbers performed at the end of a program in response to the sustained applause of the audience.

What Are Some Important Performance Customs?

Memorization

Soloists often memorize their part so that the music won't come between them and the audience. For example, a page turn can occur at a time when the performer doesn't have a hand free to turn it. Having another person turn pages can be distracting to both the audience and the performer. Operas and musicals are memorized because they are staged and the presence of sheets of music would definitely ruin the impact of a scene. Because of the number and character of the parts for chamber and orchestral music, such music is rarely memorized.

Conductors sometimes conduct without their orchestral score, but this does not mean that they have memorized every note. They know the work generally and the interpretation they want of it. This knowledge is enough for conducting it in performance.

Orchestra Concerts

Because the conductor is the leader of the performers, he or she is treated with special respect. The conductor is the last to enter and the first to leave when a long work has been completed. The audience applauds as the conductor enters. Male conductors and soloists acknowledge applause by bowing modestly. For many years female conductors and soloists curtsied, but today they usually bow.

After a work has been performed, the conductor usually recognizes the efforts of the musicians by shaking hands with the first-chair violinist in the case of a symphony orchestra. This player sits at the front of the first violin section to the conductor's left and is referred to as the concertmaster or concertmistress. Occasionally the conductor asks individual members of the group who have an important part in a work to stand and acknowledge the applause. Quite often the entire group is asked to stand to receive the recognition due them. Soloists in operas and musicals are recognized individually or in small groups in a carefully planned routine of curtain calls.

Soloists are special guests, so they are treated with even more deference than conductors. They precede the conductor on and off the stage and receive applause on their own. Incidentally, the performers applaud soloists and guest conductors, but seldom the permanent conductor.

The concertmaster participates in another tradition at orchestra concerts by being the last player to enter before the conductor. He or she then points to various sections of the orchestra, and they play a long note to tune their instruments. That tuning pitch in Europe and America is standardized: A above middle C, also known as A440 or concert A. (The random sounds you hear coming from the stage before the concertmaster arrives are simply the orchestra players warming up; not the first piece on the program!)

What's in the Printed Program?

People are usually given a printed program upon entering the concert hall listing the music that will be performed. Because programs are provided, the music is rarely announced from the stage. Programs give people who arrive early something to read, and the sale of ads provides income to the organization.

Encores are sometimes not announced. They may be just performed, apparently on the often inaccurate assumption that the audience knows them already.

Most programs list the name of the group or individual performers if there are only a few of them. On one side of the page, usually the left, the name of the composition is listed. On the other side the composer and/or arranger is given, sometimes along with the years when that person lived. Titles in foreign languages are not always translated. Each movement in a multi-movement instrumental work is usually listed by its Italian tempo marking directly under the title of the work, indicating that they are parts of the same work (remember not to clap between the movements!). For example:

Symphony No. 4 in A Major, Op. 90, "Italian"   Felix Mendelssohn (1809-1847)

> Allegro vivace
> Andante con moto
> Con moto moderato
> Saltarello; Presto

Titles in foreign languages are not always translated, but are usually provided in the program notes. Here is an example of the first two movements of *Carnival of the Animals:*

Le carnaval des animaux   Camille Saint-Saëns (1835-1921)

> Introduction et marche royale de lion
> Poules et coqs

Song recitals have programs that list each song by title and composer. Example: *Der Erlkönig* -- Franz Schubert. Oratorio programs list each important section. Opera programs look more like a program booklet for a play, listing acts and scenes and a few remarks about the time and place. Usually opera programs contain a synopsis of the action, and oratorio programs sometimes describe the setting of the story.

Programs sometimes contain notes and narrative material interspersed among the ads. These remarks may be helpful, and then again they may not. Some writers use a complex style that nonmusicians can find difficult to understand, or they may include information that is not useful.

Dress Up for Concerts?

The idea of an audience wearing fancy clothes to a concert has long since passed. In a few situations, like opening nights of the opera season in a major city, many concertgoers will dress formally, but others simply wear a suit or nice outfit. Dress is somewhat more formal for an evening concert for which admission is charged. Other performances are more casual; almost anything neat and clean is fine, but as a rule, do not wear shorts.

Do I Need to Prepare for a Performance?

The answer is both yes and no. No, you don't have to do anything ahead of time, but you will get much more out of the performance if you are at least somewhat prepared.

Preparation can begin by reviewing the portions of your text that deal with the composer or type of music you'll be hearing. For example, if you know in advance that an orchestra is going to play a symphony by Beethoven, you can look over what was said about Beethoven and his music, even though that particular symphony may not have been discussed specifically.

You will be even better prepared if you can go to a music library and listen to a recording of Beethoven's symphony and read the notes enclosed with the recording. It definitely helps to become familiar with the story of an opera and to have a copy of the libretto, especially if the opera is not in English.

Don't let concerns about inadequate musical knowledge keep you from attending performances and enjoying them. This enjoyment is not the same as going to a sports event or a theme park. It's different. Attending a concert or recital or opera is more subtle, more thoughtful, more lasting, more refined. Going to a performance can be an enriching experience in your life, and it can provide you with something that cannot be obtained in any other way. And besides - it makes for a great date!

Suggestions for Writing Concert Reports

Most concert reports will probably involve a type of narrative format in which you report on what you heard. Be sure to check the specific requirements for your particular course regarding the mechanics of the paper such as length, content, the nature of the report, and so on.

Here are some important guidelines to help you avoid a few of the more common errors that students make when writing narrative reports:

- Always submit a neat, typewritten report.

- Be sure to use correct English and mechanics of writing. Be especially careful to keep the same verb tense throughout the report!

- Do not refer to instrumental works as "songs."

- Do not use the same word like "piece" over and over, when you could use "movement" or "work" or "number" or the name or genre of the piece such as "prelude" instead.

- Make sure the title of the music (or individual movement) you are writing about is clear. This can be done through the use of italics, quotation marks, headings, underscoring, or in any manner specified by your instructor.

- Avoid trying to increase the length of your report by increasing the size of the margins or using a larger type size. Retain the normal one-inch margins and size 12 font.

- When possible, use musical terms. For example, instead of saying, "The piece got faster," write, "The tempo increased." And instead of, "He sure banged away at the piano," say, if possible, "He played with musical intensity."

- Provide the title and name of the composer or arranger for each work.

- Report on what you heard, not on the program notes, if there were any. Program notes are simply not written like a nonmusic major would write about music. Such sentences are easily detected by instructors if they appear in your report!

- You can say something about your reactions to what you heard, but do not make your feelings the major part of your report. And don't try to make your report a critique of the performance.

- Do not make vague, general remarks and do not ramble. Instead, comment directly on specific aspects of the music and the performance.

- Avoid redefining music terms or including background notes, or using extra words as fillers to expand your report! For example, **do not** write: "This piece featured the piano. The piano is a keyboard instrument that was invented in Italy in 1709 by Bartolemo Cristofori. It wasn't used a whole lot until the Classical period. But what's known as the Golden Age of the Piano didn't occur until the nineteenth century. The piano is really a popular instrument, that's why I like it. Lots of groups use piano, but mostly they use electronic keyboards."

Instructors want to know that you attended the entire concert and that you made an honest attempt to listen carefully to the music. If you do this and follow your specific guidelines as well as those just presented when writing your report, you will have fulfilled the intent of the concert-going experience.

PART I

The Nature of Music

The difference between music and random sounds or noise is that in music the sounds are organized. Music can be defined as: *Organized sounds occurring within a prescribed span of time.* The random noises you might hear while standing on a street corner do not fulfill that definition, but organized sounds, even though they may seem unpleasant, do. Organized sounds may meet the minimum definition of music, but not be anything you want to listen to again. That's a matter of personal preference, which is based on a person's experience with and knowledge of music.

Sound is made up of vibrations of molecules in the air. When vibrations are transmitted to our ears, we perceive them as sound.

Each musical sound always has three characteristics:

1. Duration (length of the sound)
2. Dynamic level (degree of loudness)
3. Timbre (tone color or source of the sound)

And almost all musical sounds have a fourth:

4. Pitch (high or low)

In music, the combination of sounds are organized according to elements such as rhythm, melody, harmony, form, dynamics, timbre, and texture. Each chapter in this first part can help you understand better the organization of musical sounds.

Chapter 1 Review

Music Listening and You

Main Points

1. Music is important to the quality of human life. It is one of the things that makes the difference between living a fuller life and just existing.

2. People have created different types of music for different purposes.

3. Art music, or concert music is music created for the intellectual and psychological satisfaction it provides. It is one area of the fine arts.

4. Usually people like the kinds of music they are familiar with. But there is a vast treasure of music in addition to the ones a person happens to know and like.

5. Try using different modes of listening (sensuous, expressive, and sheerly musical)

6. You can learn to listen to music more perceptively if you:

- Realize that hearing and listening are not the same thing.
- Listen for the musical features in each piece.
- Develop different modes of listening.
- Develop different expectations that are appropriate for different types of music.
- Improve your musical memory.
- Become more sensitive to musical sounds.
- Use the Active Listening Guides and the listening guides in the text to help gain greater listening skill.

7. The main goal of a music appreciation course is to provide you with a basic understanding of the language and literature of music in its various cultural and historical contexts through active listening. It should enable you to:

- Increase your ability to listen to music perceptively
- Acquire basic, useful information about music
- Develop a greater familiarity with all types of music

Musical Terms

> art music, concert music
> fine arts
> coda

Chapter 2 Review

Rhythm

Main Points

1. All music takes place in a span of time. The term for the flow of music through time is rhythm.

2. Beat is the underlying steady pulse in music. It's what you march or dance to, and is found in almost all music in Western civilization. Beats are also the units of measurement in keeping track of musical time. Note values indicate length in terms of the beat and follow a 2:1 ratio.

3. Meter is the pattern created by accented and unaccented beats. Patterns usually occur in twos, threes, or fours, but others are also encountered.

4. In music notation these patterns are shown by vertical lines called bars, which create units called measures. Two numbers are placed at the beginning of a piece, called the time signature or meter signature. They indicate the number of beats in a measure and what type of note receives the beat.

5. Tempo is the term for the speed of the beats. It is indicated either by words (usually in Italian) or by a metronome marking.

6. Syncopation occurs when the rhythmic emphasis shifts to where it is not expected, or is absent when it is expected.

7. Polyrhythm is created by two or more rhythmic patterns occurring at the same time.

Musical Terms

rhythm	meter signature; time signature
beat	syncopation
accent	tempo
meter; metrical	polyrhythm
downbeat	allegro
presto	andante
vivace	adagio

Chapter 3 Review

Melody and Harmony

Main Points

1. Almost all music involves pitch, which is the degree of how high or low a note sounds.

2. Sound is made up of vibrations of molecules in the air. Pitch is determined by the number of vibrations per second. The greater the number of vibrations (frequency), the higher the pitch, and vice versa.

3. Pitches are written on a staff of five lines and four spaces. Notes written higher on the staff sound higher in pitch, while those written lower sound lower in pitch.

4. Symbols called clefs are placed at the beginning of each line of music to determine the exact pitches of notes. The treble clef (𝄞) and bass clef (𝄢) are the most commonly used clef signs. Notes are raised one half step when a sharp (♯) is placed in front of them, and lowered one half step when preceded by a flat (♭).

5. A melody is a series of consecutive pitches sounded one after another that are cohesive. Melodies contain cadences or musical resting places that allow the singer or instrumentalist to breathe. The word "tune" also refers to melody. A theme is an important melody that is often developed within a musical work.

6. Melodies have several characteristics:

- length (short or long)
- range (narrow or wide)
- movement (by step or by leap)
- contour (the shape or outline)
- plain or with ornamentation (decorative notes) added

7. Harmony is the simultaneous sounding of notes that are not melodies. It may sound pleasant (consonant) or tense and harsh (dissonant). Harmony gives the piece an appropriate setting.

8. Chords are three or more notes sounded together. Most chords in Western music are based on the interval of a third, which means that the notes are arranged in an every-other pattern--A-C-E, and so on.

9. Most music we are familiar with centers around a home pitch and the chord based on that note. This home pitch is called the key or tonic. Music is said to be in a key or tonality.

10. Changing the key within a musical work is called modulation. Music generally moves away from and then back to its original key.

11. Scales are series of stepwise pitches that ascend or descend according to a definite pattern. They are the skeleton around which melodies and chords are built.

12. Major chords and tonalities generally have a brighter quality while minor ones tend to be heavier and sometimes solemn. But other aspects of a musical work can change the quality of the music very much.

13. Texture refers to the basic use of pitch in music; whether the music is conceived more in terms of melodic lines or simultaneous sounds. There are three basic textures in music:

- monophonic (one melody alone)
- homophonic (melody with accompaniment)
- polyphonic (two or more melodies sounded together at the same time)

14. Counterpoint (or polyphony) occurs when either the same melody is sounded in imitation, like a canon or round, or when two different melodies are sounded together.

Musical Terms

pitch
staff
clef
sharp; flat
melody
phrases
theme
harmony
consonant (consonance)
dissonant (dissonance)
counterpoint
imitation; canon; round
texture

chord
Interval
octave
tonality; tonal center
key
cadence
modulation
scale
major/minor
monophonic (monophony)
homophonic (homophony)
polyphonic (polyphony)

Chapter 4 Review

Dynamics, Timbre, and Organization

<u>Main Points</u>

1. All sounds have a degree of strength or loudness, otherwise they couldn't be heard. The term for the degrees of loudness is dynamics. Words that describe loudness are general, and they are traditionally Italian terms. Soft is indicated by the word "piano" and loud by the word "forte," but these terms are often modified. They are abbreviated to just letters in music notation: *p* for piano and *f* for forte.

2. Gradual changes of dynamic level are indicated by cresc. for crescendo, or the symbol $<$, meaning the music should become louder. The opposite is decresc. for decrescendo, or the symbol $>$, meaning the music should get softer. Another word for decrescendo is diminuendo.

3. Timbre refers to the tone quality of an instrument or voice. Timbres vary according to the number and strength of the partials sounding in the overtone series.

4. The overtone series is a phenomenon of nature. It is the pattern of pitches that results when dividing a string or column of air at fractional points.

5. Music is the result of its various elements being organized. Often musical works are organized according to forms. Forms are constructed around one or more of three general considerations:

- repetition
- variation
- contrast

6. A favorite musical effect is the contrast between groups of instruments, or what is called concerted style. A concerto is a piece that features a solo instrumentalist with an orchestra. Cadenzas are played by the soloist alone.

7. Letters are used to designate forms. These letters appear in italics. Upper case letters are used for the main sections of a work. Lower case letters are used for

shorter sections of music. The prime sign (') is used after a letter to indicate that it is slightly modified from the original.

Musical Terms

dynamics
forte; *f*
piano; *p*
crescendo
decrescendo
timbre
music

partials; overtone series
form
motive
concerto
cadenza
movement
genre

Chapter 5 Review

Orchestral Instruments

Main Points

1. All musical instruments can be examined by looking at four things. How they:

- produce sound
- modify their basic timbre
- produce different pitches
- start and stop their sounds

2. The instruments in a symphony orchestra are classified into four basic groups or families: strings, woodwinds, brasses, and percussion. There are approximately 100 players in a symphony orchestra.

3. Strings: String instruments include (from the smallest and highest to the largest and lowest): the violin, viola, cello, and double bass, plus the harp. They produce sound when their strings are plucked (pizzicato) or bowed. The vibrations of the string are resonated through a mostly hollow body.

4. String players (except harpists) modify their sound by vibrating their left hand (vibrato) and the manner in which they draw the bow across the string. The pitch is determined by which string is played and where the finger is placed on the string, which regulates the amount of string allowed to vibrate. Players stop and start sounds with the bow or when they pluck a string.

5. Woodwinds: Woodwind instruments (clarinet, oboe, and bassoon) are made of wood. The exception is the flute, which today is made of metal. Woodwinds produce sound when air is blown through them. All woodwinds use one or two reeds to produce their tones except the flute (and piccolo). For these two instruments, air is blown into a mouthpiece and the collision of air streams produces the sounds. Each woodwind instrument has its own distinct timbre.

6. Except for the clarinet, woodwind players can modify their timbre through the use of vibrato. Sounds on woodwinds are stopped and started by the player's tongue. The pitch depends on which holes are covered or which keys are opened.

7. Brasses: Brass instruments (trumpet, French horn, trombone, and tuba) are all made of metal. They all produce sound by the vibration of the player's lip membranes as air is blown into a cup-shaped mouthpiece. Brasses are considered to be a type of wind instrument.

8. All brass instruments can modify their sounds through the use of mutes (and the player's hand in the case of the French horn) and vibrato. Sounds are stopped and started when the player's tongue opens and closes the air stream going through the lips. The pitch depends on a combination of lip tension (which determines which part of the overtone series is used), and the amount of tubing the player has engaged through the use of valves or a slide.

9. Percussion: Percussion instruments are those that produce sounds when struck, usually with a stick or a mallet, or shaken. All start and stop their sounds when struck. They can be classified into those that produce a definite pitch (timpani, xylophone, bells, marimba) and those that do not (snare drum, cymbals, wood block, gong, and others).

10. Pitched percussion instruments like the xylophone have bars arranged like a keyboard; the pitch depends on which bar is struck. The pitch of the timpani can be changed by the amount of tension in the heads of the drums, which is regulated by a pedal mechanism. The sounds of percussion instruments can be modified by the manner in which they are struck and the type of stick used.

Musical Terms

symphony orchestra; 4 families of instruments
string instruments
> violin, viola, cello, double bass, harp

woodwind instruments
> flute, clarinet, oboe, bassoon

brass instruments
> trumpet, French horn, trombone, tuba

percussion instruments
> pitched and nonpitched

vibrato
mute
pizzicato
harmonics

Chapter 6 Review

Other Musical Instruments

Main Points

1. The voice is a musical instrument. It has its own means of producing and modifying sound. The standard ranges of the voice from highest to lowest are soprano, alto, tenor, and bass.

2. A wind band consists of only wind and percussion instruments, except for one string bass. It also includes several sizes of saxophones, baritone horns, and alto clarinets.

3. The most prominent keyboard instruments are the piano, harpsichord, and pipe organ. Depressing the keys of the piano causes felt hammers to strike the strings. Its earlier name, the pianoforte, was derived from the fact that the player can vary the dynamic level by how forcefully the keys are depressed.

4. The harpsichord produces sound when depressing the key causes the string to be plucked. Dynamic contrast is achieved by changing from one to the other of its keyboards (manuals) or by coupling them together.

5. The pipe organ operates from a keyboard, including a pedalboard that is played with the feet. Its sounds are created when air is blown through its many pipes.

6. Electronic instruments can be divided into two basic groups:

   - instruments that acoustically alter or amplify sounds (electric guitar and electronic drums, for example)
   - synthesizers and computers that create music.

A major change that has occurred in these instruments over the decades has been from analog to digitally produced sounds; from the use of continuous sounds to processing separate numbers. To enhance sound quality synthesizers can store recorded samples of actual complex instrumental sounds for later use in a composition. This process is called sampling.

Musical Terms

vocal types
     soprano, alto, tenor, bass
wind band; concert band
keyboard instruments
     piano: upright and grand
     harpsichord
pipe organ
     manuals
     ranks
     pedalboard
popular instruments
     guitar
     accordion
electronic instruments; acoustic instruments
analog sound production
digital sound production
sampling

NOTABLE FEATURES OF THE NATURE OF MUSIC

- Music is one thing that makes the difference between living and existing
- Perceptive listening can be developed through careful practice
- Music flows through time, so all music has rhythm of some type
- Beat, meter, and tempo are aspects of rhythm
- Four basic elements of music are pitch, rhythm, dynamics and timbre
- Pitches are used in music to form melodies, counterpoint, and harmony
- There are three textures of music -- monophonic, polyphonic, homophonic
- Dynamics are the differing levels of loudness in music
- All instruments and each human voice have their own timbre or tone quality
- Form in music is created through the use of repetition, variation, and contrast
- Orchestral instruments are divided into four families: strings, woodwinds, brasses, and percussion
- The piano, harpsichord, and pipe organ are the most important keyboard instruments
- Digital sound is created by processing separate numbers

Discussion and Critical Thinking

1. Why should college students learn about music that is _not_ their favorite type?

2. Rodrigo was undergoing a difficult time in his life when he wrote *Concierto de Aranjuez.* What do you think he was trying to express in the second movement of this piece?

Part I Review Questions

These questions are a review of information and terminology using three different formats: matching, crossword puzzle, and multiple choice. The answers are found on pages 36 - 38.

Matching. Match each term with its correct definition by placing the appropriate letter in the space provided.

O	1. Melody	I	14. Counterpoint	
H	2. Rhythm	L	15. Dynamics	
S	3. Meter	U	16. Tonality	
Q	4. Consonance	X	17. Homophonic A F
Z	5. Concerto	G	18. Timbre	
F	6. Polyphonic	M	19. Chord	
R	7. Cadence	P	20. Beat	
C	8. Music C.	B	21. Dissonance B.
J	9. Cadenza	T	22. Tempo	
N	10. Pitch	V	23. Monophonic	
E	11. Modulation	Y	24. Motive	
K	12. Crescendo D.	A	25. Polyrhythm	
D	13. Forte	W	26. Accent	

DEFINITIONS

A.   Two or more rhythmic patterns occurring simultaneously

B.   A group of simultaneous sounds that seems disagreeable or harsh

C.   Organized sounds occurring in a prescribed span of time

D.   Italian term meaning loud

E.   Changing the tonal center as the music progresses, usually without a break

F.   Two or more melodies sounded together at the same time

G.   Tone quality or tone color in music

H.   The flow of music in terms of time

I.   Two or more independent lines with melodic character occurring at the same time

J.   Free-sounding section of a concerto where the soloist plays alone

K.   Italian term meaning to increase in volume; gradually become louder

L.   The degree of loudness in music

M.   The simultaneous sounding of three or more pitches

N.   The degree of high or low sounds

O.   A series of consecutive pitches that form a unified musical whole

P.   The basic pulse that underlies the rhythm and recurs regularly in music

Q.   A group of simultaneous sounds that seems agreeable or restful

R.   A melodic or harmonic formula that gives a sense of ending or rest

S.   The pattern of stressed and unstressed beats

T.   The speed of the beats

U.   Centering notes around one particular pitch

V.   Texture consisting of one melodic line alone without any accompaniment

W.   The emphasis placed on a note, usually by playing it louder

X.   Texture consisting of melody with accompaniment

Y.   Short recurring melodic or rhythmic idea, used often in a musical work

Z.   Multimovement work that contrasts a soloist with an orchestra or band

Elements of Music

www.CrosswordWeaver.com

ACROSS

3 tune
8 harsh sounds
10 two or more rhythmic patterns at the same time
13 soft
15 large independent section of an instrumental work
19 melody with accompaniment
21 multi-movement work featuring a soloist with orchestra
27 pattern of the beats
29 another name for key
31 changing tonality
32 lines and spaces that music is written on
34 unexpected accent
35 accompanying chords
37 short recurring melodic or rhythmic idea
38 gradually get softer

DOWN

1 closing progression
2 organized sounds
4 eight notes higher or lower
5 steady pulse
6 pattern or plan of a musical work
7 speed of the beats
9 emphasis
10 degree of high or low sounds
11 melody alone
12 polyphonic texture
14 agreeable sounds
16 three or more pitches sounded together
17 main melody
18 tone quality
20 distance between two notes
22 series
23 solo passages in a concerto
24 sharps, flats, naturals
25 degree of loud
26 flow of music through time
28 gradually get louder
30 series of stepwise notes
33 loud
36 another name for tonality

Musical Instruments

www.CrosswordWeaver.com

ACROSS

2 electronic sounds produced on tape or disc in continuous motion
4 keyboard instrument that plucks the strings
6 lowest female voice
9 lowest male voice
10 keyboard instrument with a pedalboard
13 instruments that make sounds only when struck or shaken
15 instruments; acoustic instruments
17 highest male voice
21 highest female voice
22 instrument that uses a slide to change pitch
27 keyboard instrument that makes sounds when felt hammers strike the strings
29 type of piano in which the strings are laid parallel to the floor
30 drums
31 another name for orchestra

DOWN

1 an instrument that has frets

2 instruments that are blown into
3 woodwind instrument that uses a single reed
5 family of instruments originally made of wood
7 plucked strings
8 string instrument with foot pedals and played witout a bow
11 used by string and brass players to soften the sound and modify timbre
12 small, rapid fluctuations of pitch
14 instrument invented by Adolphe Sax
16 instruments that produce sound from a vibrating string
18 musical instrument that every person is born with
19 percussion instruments other than drums
20 woodwind instrument that doesn't use a reed
23 woodwind instrument that uses a double reed
24 instrumental group with no strings
25 highest and smallest string instrument
26 instruments that play only notes of the overtone series
28 largest and lowest pitched brass instrument

Multiple Choice. Circle the correct answer.

1. The main contribution of music to people's lives is
   a. physical (b.) psychological c. religious d. All of the above

2. Three ways or modes of listening to music are
   a. sensuous, literal, and passive
   (b.) sensuous, expressive, and purely musical
   c. expressive, purely musical, and as accompaniment to activity
   d. purely musical, fantasizing, and sensuous
   e. literal, active, and purely musical

3. Because music is an art that exists in time, it is good to
   a. let your mind wander as you listen
   (b.) focus on the themes and try to remember them
   c. visualize scenes to the tunes
   d. use music as a background to mask other sounds

4. Meter is
   a. the number of beats in a measure
   b. the type of note that receives one beat
   c. the pattern of the notes
   (d.) the pattern of the beats
   e. the speed of the beats

5. The terms for the different tempos in music are usually in
   a. French   b. Latin   c. German   d. English   (e.) Italian

6. The term for two melodies of approximately equal interest sounding at the same time is
   (a.) counterpoint   b. harmony   c. polyrhythm   d. melodious
   e. accompaniment

7. Homophonic texture is basically
   a. two melodies sounded at the same time
   b. one melody sounded alone without accompaniment
   (c.) a melody with accompanying parts
   d. a melody with a smooth contour
   e. several series of chords that sound pleasing

8. A texture featuring a single unaccompanied melodic line is called:
   (a.) monophonic   b. homophonic   c. polyphonic   d. monody
   e. None of the above

9. Timbre refers to
   a. the length of a tone
   b. the pitch of a tone
   c. the color or quality of a tone
   d. the sound of a tree falling

10. Which is not one of the four basic elements of most musical sounds?
    a. pitch   b. texture   c. loudness   d. timbre   e. duration

11. Which of these dynamic markings is the softest?
    a. pianissimo (*pp*)   b. fortissimo (*ff*)   c. piano (*p*)   d. forte (*f*)
    e. mezzo piano (*mp*)

12. The overtone or harmonic series refers to the
    a. loudest pitches in a chord
    b. loudest pitches in a melody
    c. pattern of pitches that results when dividing a string or air column at
    fractional points
    d. notes of the minor scale
    e. different dynamic levels

13. One of the differences between musical sounds and ordinary sounds is that
    in music the sounds
    a. harmonize well together
    b. sound pretty
    c. are organized
    d. are spontaneous

14. Which is the correct order of bowed string instruments from highest to
    lowest?
    a. viola, violin, cello, bass
    b. violin, viola, cello, bass
    c. bass, cello, viola, violin
    d. violin, cello, viola, bass

15. Bowed string instruments can add warmth to the sound by using
    a. amplification   b. vibrato   c. resonance   d. double stops
    e. harmonics

16. Woodwind instruments
    a. all use reeds
    b. all involve blowing into the instrument
    c. all are made of wood
    d. all have the same fingering system

17. Which percussion instrument can play different pitches?
    a. snare drum   b. bass drum   c. cymbals   d. tambourine
    e. timpani

18. How does a singer regulate pitch?
    a. By varying the amount of air used
    b. By adjusting the tension in the vocal cords
    c. By changing the formation of the lips and tongue
    d. By altering the speed of the air going through the vocal cords
    e. By how wide the mouth is open

19. The difference between a band and an orchestra is
    a. an orchestra does not have a bass drum
    b. a band has no violins or cellos
    c. a band does not have woodwinds
    d. an orchestra does not have a tuba
    e. All of these choices

20. Musical texture refers to the use of
    a. rhythm
    b. harmony
    c. form
    d. pitch

Answers to Matching Review Questions

1 – O	14 – I
2 – H	15 – L
3 – S	16 – U
4 – Q	17 – X
5 – Z	18 – G
6 – F	19 – M
7 – R	20 – P
8 – C	21 – B
9 – J	22 – T
10 - N	23 – V
11 - E	24 – Y
12 - K	25 – A
13 - D	26 – W

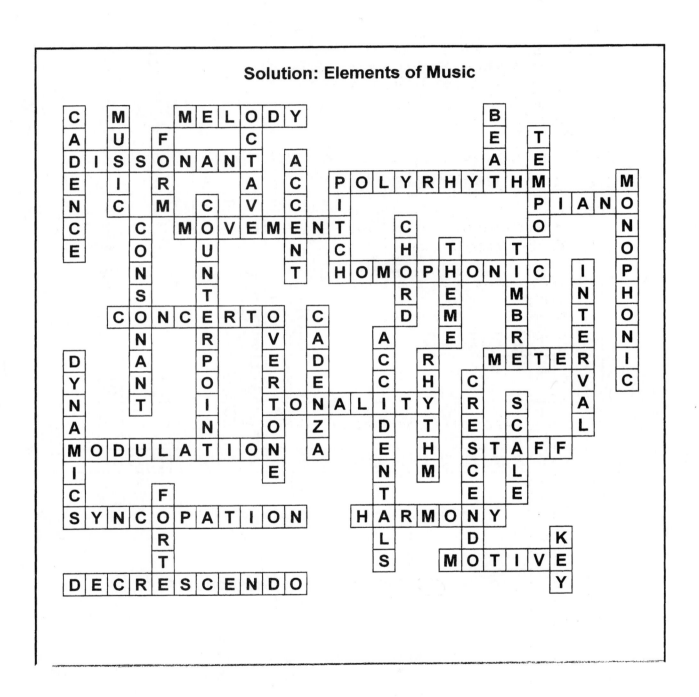

Solution: Elements of Music

Solution: Musical Instruments

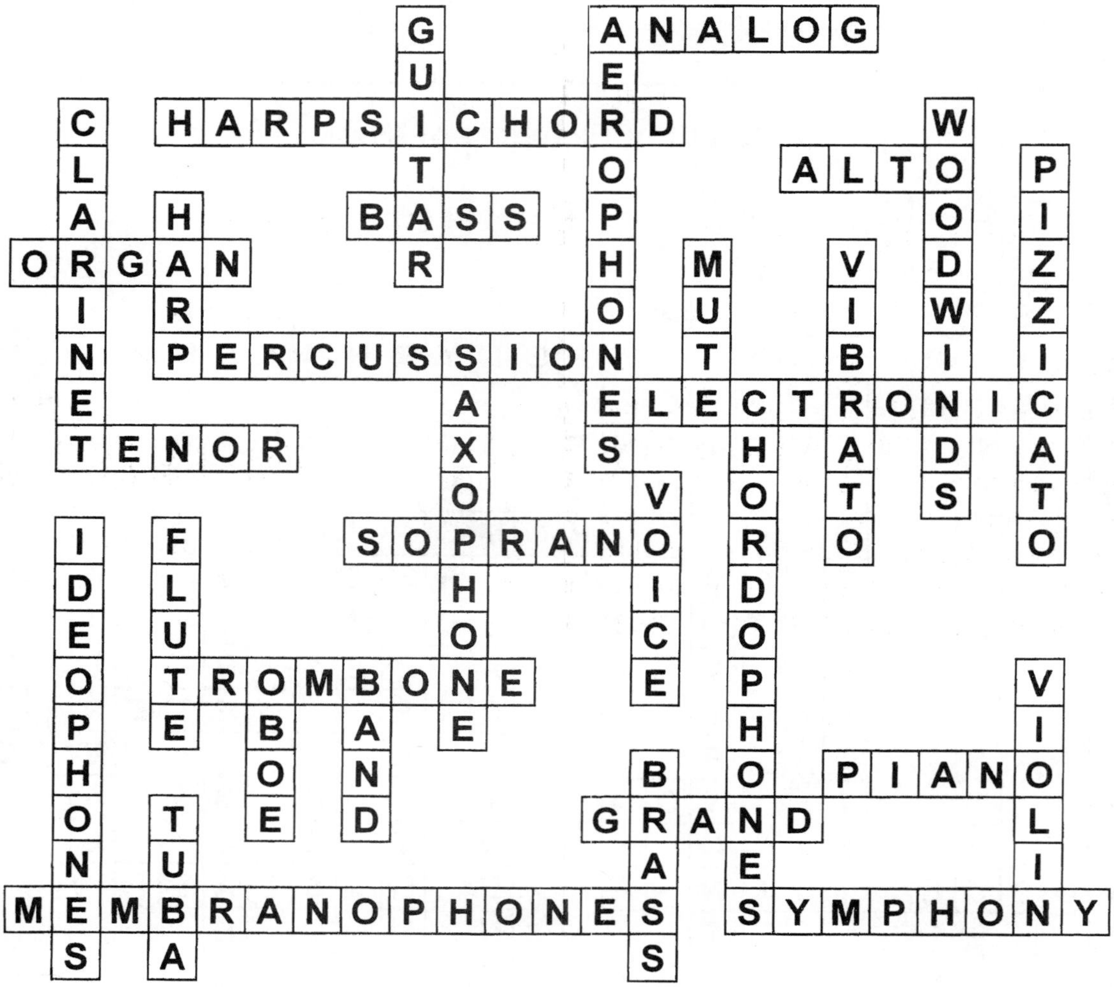
ANALOG
GUITAR
AEROPHONES
HARPSICHORD
CLARINET
WOODWINDS
ALTO
PIZZICATO
HARP
BASS
ORGAN
MUTE
VIBRATO
PERCUSSION
SAXOPHONE
ELECTRONIC
TENOR
CHORDOPHONES
VOICE
IDEOPHONES
FLUTE
SOPRANO
TROMBONE
OBOE
BAND
VIOLIN
BRASS
PIANO
GRAND
TUBA
MEMBRANOPHONES
SYMPHONY

Answers to Multiple Choice Questions

1 – B	6 - A	11 – A	16 - B
2 – B	7 - C	12 – C	17 - E
3 – B	8 - A	13 – C	18 - B
4 – D	9 - C	14 – B	19 - B
5 – E	10 - B	15 – B	20 - D

PART II

Early, Medieval, and Renaissance Music

Music has existed since the beginning of civilization. It is found in every part of the globe throughout the thousands of years that human beings have been around. But until the development of music notation, and especially since the advent of recordings, it was not possible to know exactly how music sounded. Therefore, not much can be said about early music, even though we know through literature and art that it existed and was important to people. Early music was used in connection with various functions (religious rituals, ceremonial dances, war dances, and so forth).

Chapter 7 Review

Early Western Music

Main Points

1. As far as can be determined, there has been music since the dawn of history. But we have only verbal descriptions and pictures to tell us about it.

2 . From about 800 B.C. to 476 A.D. Western civilization was dominated by various city states around the Mediterranean Sea. Greece, especially Athens, was most important during the early centuries of these years, and then the Roman Empire ruled. This was a time of great accomplishments in the arts and philosophy.

3. Pythagoras found that certain intervals found in the overtone series can be represented in mathematical ratios such as 2:1 and 3:2.

4. The only type of music we know much about is the sacred music for the Roman Catholic Church, which was written down and preserved in monasteries. Around the year 1000 a system of square notes on a four-line staff was created.

5. Worship in the Christian church grew out of Judaism. It assumed many of the Jewish religious practices such as daily prayer hours and the singing of psalms.

6. Church music, called Gregorian chant, was compiled and codified about the sixth century under a directive from Pope Gregory. Particular chants were assigned to certain days of the church calendar.

7. The most important form of worship in the Roman Catholic Church is the Mass. It consists of two different types of prayers, the Proper and the Ordinary. Prayers included in the Proper change daily according to the church calendar. The parts of the Ordinary are sung or spoken at every Mass. They are the Kyrie, Gloria, Credo, Sanctus, and Agnus Dei. The Ordinary is what composers set to music.

8. A Requiem is a Roman Catholic funeral Mass. It includes the "Dies irae" chant (which translated means "Day of Wrath" in reference to the final judgment).

9. Gregorian chant differs from the music most people know today. Chant is:

- monophonic
- has no accompaniment

- sung in Latin
- sung by monks and priests
- nonmetrical; it does not have a strong beat, but is gentle and free flowing
- often sung with one syllable sustained for many notes
- modal; does not use the familiar major/minor keys
- conjunct (a smooth, stepwise melody) and has a narrow range
- intended for worship; it projects an attitude of reverence

10. A number of musical morality plays were created. Their main purpose was to educate the listeners about the Christian faith.

Musical Terms

Gregorian chant
Mass
    Proper
    Ordinary of the Mass
        Kyrie
        Gloria
        Credo
        Sanctus
        Agnus Dei
Requiem
Dies irae
morality play

Chapter 8 Review

Medieval Music

Main Points

1. The Medieval period lasted from about 1100-1450. It was the time of Scholasticism and when many great cathedrals were built. The period was also marked by chivalry, guilds, and the founding of universities. Many works of art were created anonymously.

2. Organum consisted of parallel lines of Gregorian chant that were a fourth or fifth apart.

3. The earliest polyphony developed at the Cathedral of Notre Dame in Paris when a third and fourth line were added and parts became more independent. The music was based on a phrase of Gregorian chant, often sung in long notes like a drone.

4. Rhythmic modes, much like the meters found in poetry, were used to help keep the different parts together.

5. The medieval motet was a complicated vocal work that developed in France. It was built around a phrase of Gregorian chant called the cantus firmus, which was sung in Latin in long notes.

4. Other melodies were added above the cantus firmus in French or Italian, and their texts could be love songs or something else unrelated to the words of the cantus firmus. Complicated rhythmic or melodic schemes were worked into the music. The medieval motet disappeared by end of the period.

5. Secular music existed, but little of it was written down. Some dance music for instrumental groups survived.

Musical Terms

        Medieval motet
        organum
        secular music
        rhythmic modes
        cantus firmus
        drone

Chapter 9 Review

Renaissance Music

Main Points

1, The word Renaissance means "rebirth." During this time there was a renewed interest in the culture of ancient Greece and Rome. An attitude of humanism prevailed, with an interest in the arts.

2. The Renaissance was the age of great explorers like Balboa and Magellan, advances in science and literature, and the invention of the printing press by Gutenburg.

3. The bass voice part was an important addition to the choral settings of Masses and motets, many of which were built on a phrase of Gregorian chant.

4. The Renaissance motet was quite different from a medieval motet. The Renaissance motet:

- is a sacred work
- is sung in Latin
- has a sacred text – all voices sing the same words
- has a polyphonic texture, with one voice part following another
- introduces new phrases of text in imitation, so that the words could be more clearly heard
- is written for small choirs of about eight or so singers; only men and boys sang in church during this time.
- does not have a strong feeling of meter or beat; the original editions of motets did not have any bar lines
- is sung a cappella today, but during the Renaissance the voice parts were sometimes doubled by instruments

4. The madrigal was the best-known type of secular vocal music composed during the Renaissance. Madrigals are similar to motets in several ways. They are:

- written for small groups
- usually polyphonic, although some portions of them are chordal
- sung a cappella
- melodic, with smooth, singable vocal lines

But a madrigal is different from a motet in other ways, because a madrigal:

- is a secular work
- is sung in vernacular languages (English, Italian, etc.), not Latin
- was originally sung at courtly gatherings and meetings of learned societies
- is performed by both men and women
- has texts that are often about sentimental and sometimes erotic love
- contains word painting to project particular words or thoughts
- has metrical rhythm
- is usually performed at a faster tempo

5. Some instrumental music existed during the Renaissance, especially for the lute.

Musical Terms

Renaissance
motet
a cappella
madrigal
word painting; text painting
secular music
chanson
polyphonic
imitation

NOTABLE FEATURES OF RENAISSANCE MUSIC

- Sacred vocal music predominates
- A cappella singing
- Polyphonic texture
- Small performing groups
- Restrained, intimate style
- Sacred genres: (sung in Latin) Mass, motet
- Secular genres: (sung in vernacular languages) Italian and English madrigals; French chansons
- Text painting
- Use of cantus firmus

Discussion and Critical Thinking

1. What is the function of Gregorian chant? How does that function affect who performs it and the way in which it is performed? For what audience is chant intended?

2. What characteristics of humanism are evident in the madrigal? How does the motet manifest the ideal of religious reverence?

3. Is text painting more prominent in sacred or secular vocal music? What do you think is the reason?

Part II Review Questions

These questions are a review of information and terminology using two different formats: matching and multiple choice. The answers are found on page 50.

Matching. Match each term with its correct definition by placing the appropriate letter in the space provided.

_____ 1. Madrigal	_____ 9. Rhythmic modes
_____ 2. Morality play	_____ 10. Secular music
_____ 3. Drone	_____ 11. Mass
_____ 4. A cappella	_____ 12. Dies irae
_____ 5. Motet	_____ 13. Word painting
_____ 6. Cantus firmus	_____ 14. Gregorian chant
_____ 7. Chanson	_____ 15. Requiem
_____ 8. Organum	_____ 16. Imitation

DEFINITIONS

A. Roman Catholic funeral Mass
B. A polyphonic, sacred choral composition
C. Celebration of the Eucharist in the Roman Catholic Church; musical setting of the Ordinary of the Mass
D. A steady, continuous sound
E. French polyphonic song of the 17th century
F. Traditional religious theme meaning "Day of Wrath;" taken from the medieval Mass for the dead
G. A secular, imitative work for voices associated with the Renaissance
H. The liturgical chant of the Roman Catholic Church; also known as plainsong
I. Unaccompanied choral music

J.   Music that is worldly or nonsacred
K. A preexisting melody used as the basis for a polyphonic vocal work
L.   Constant repetition of certain rhythmic patterns, similar to poetic meters
M. Parallel lines of Gregorian chant a fourth or fifth apart
N. Repetition of a theme in another part or line a few beats later
O. Technique of having the music represent the words being sung
P. Vocal Medieval play created to educate the listeners about Christianity

Multiple Choice.   Circle the correct answer.

1. The Medieval period
     a. preceded the Roman Empire
     b. featured an otherworldly outlook of life
     c. saw an outburst of interest in the arts
     d. showed much interest in ancient Greek culture

2. The person who discovered the mathematical ratio of sounds was
     a. St. Thomas Aquinas   b. Guido d'Arezzo   c. Pythagoras   d. Plato
     e. Pope Gregory

3. The "Dies irae" is a Gregorian chant sung at
     a. sunrise   b. sunset   c. funerals   d. weddings   e. baptisms

4. A feature of Gregorian chant is
     a. the Italian text
     b. strict metrical rhythm
     c. singing in two parts
     d. little counterpoint
     e. monophonic texture

5. What is different about the devil's part in Hildegard's morality play *Ordo virtutum?*
     a. It constantly sings the same pitch.
     b. It is sung in falsetto (false voice).
     c. It is in a low range.
     d. It follows a metrical pattern.
     e. It is spoken, not sung

6. A Medieval motet was built on a phrase of Gregorian chant called the
     a. ground bass   b. Dies irae   c. cantus firmus   d. superius   e. maximus

7. A feature of Renaissance motets is
    a. imitation when new lines of text are introduced
    b. voice parts sung in Latin and another language
    c. complex rhythms and melodies
    d. the vigorous rendition of important words in the text
    e. monophonic texture

8. Which statement is <u>true</u> about Renaissance motets?
    a. Usually sung by large choirs
    b. Dynamic levels were loud
    c. The singing was a cappella
    d. The melodies were often ornamented

9. According to your text, which characteristic is true regarding troubadour music? Troubadour music is:
    a. sacred
    b. sung in Latin
    c. secular
    d. for a small group of singers

10. The motets of Machaut contain
    a. metrical rhythm
    b. complex compositional devices
    c. a bass vocal part
    d. instrumental accompaniment

Early, Medieval, and Renaissance

www.CrosswordWeaver.com

ACROSS

4 part of the Mass that changes daily
7 celebration of Last Supper
9 type of Medieval mode similar to meters in poetry
10 sacred polyphonic choral work
12 two or more melodic lines
13 same melody in follow-the-leader fashion
14 continuous sound
15 secular vocal work

DOWN

1 type of play composed to educate listeners about the Christian faith
2 part of Ordinary of the Mass
3 parallel lines of chant
5 rebirth
6 6th Century Pope who codified and compiled chant
8 not sacred
9 Mass for the dead
11 Gregorian

Answers to Matching Review Questions

1 - G	9 - L
2 - P	10 - J
3 - D	11 - C
4 - I	12 - F
5 - B	13 - O
6 - K	14 - H
7 - E	15 - A
8 - M	16 - N

Answers to Multiple Choice Questions

1 – B	6 – C
2 – C	7 – A
3 – C	8 – C
4 – E	9 – C
5 – E	10 – B

Solution: Early, Medieval, and Renaissance

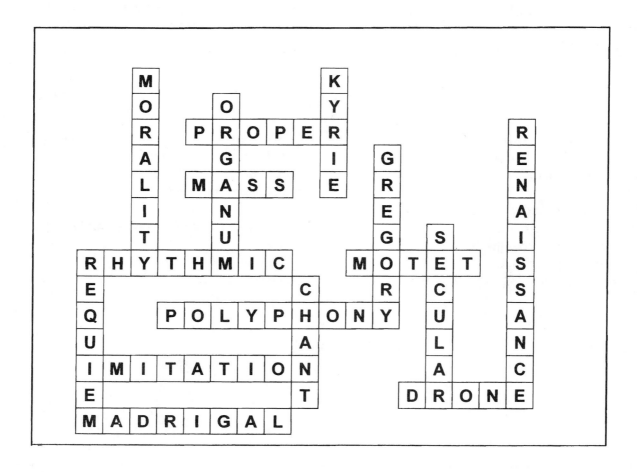

PART III

Baroque Music

Even before 1600, the approximate beginning of the Baroque period, a new style had been emerging. The Renaissance ideals of restraint and balance began to fade. The change could be seen in the growing emotion displayed in the later works of Michelangelo, and it could be heard in Giovanni Gabrieli's works for instruments and two choruses. The initial reaction to the new style is found in the word *baroque* itself, which was probably derived from a Portuguese word meaning "irregularly shaped pearl."

Sometimes *baroque* means extravagant, grotesque, and in bad taste, which is likely a carryover from its original meaning. In discussions of music and art, however, "Baroque" refers only to the style that prevailed from about 1600 to 1750. And that style was certainly not grotesque or in bad taste.

Chapter 10 Review

The Baroque Period

Main Points

1. Three characteristics stand out about Baroque thinking, especially in the arts:

    *   Grandiose – Baroque artists and musicians tended to think big. They created large buildings, pieces of sculpture, and paintings. The pipe organ, the mightiest musical instrument of its time, was developed.

    *   Dramatic – Baroque artists and musicians infused drama into their works. Painters such as Rembrandt spotlighted portions of their paintings that combined with the dark background to produce a very dramatic effect. Calm, straight lines of the Renaissance gave way to dramatic, twisted, and emotional figures.

    *   Religious – The intense religious feelings of the time affected all the arts.

2. The Baroque was a time of major scientific advances including Newton's theory of gravity, Descartes' founding of analytical geometry, and Galileo's contributions to astronomy.

3. Polychoral or antiphonal music reached a peak in the early seventeenth century with its powerful stereophonic sound provided by one group of performers answering the other from opposite sides of the church.

4. Three major dramatic musical genres were developed: opera, oratorio, and cantata.

5. Many Baroque composers worked under a patronage arrangement in which they composed music exclusively for their employer. Because no repertoire of works yet existed, they had to compose enormous amounts of new music.

6. Improvisation was very important in the performances of Baroque music.

7. Homophonic texture was developed and existed equally with polyphonic texture. In homophonic music the outer voices (the melody and the bass) are more important than the inner parts.

8. Baroque harmony was built around a tonal center and the systematic use of chords. Major and minor keys replaced the modes. Modulations became common.

9. The Doctrine of Affections was a belief about the emotional and affective qualities of music. It was thought that an entire work or section of a work should have one consistent mood.

10. Baroque composers often attempted to depict the words of the text in the notes of the music, as composers had sometimes done in Renaissance madrigals.

11. Recitative singing emphasizes the expression of the text. Because of this, recitatives are not very melodious. They are usually sung with flexible rhythm and simple accompanying music.

12. Equal temperament solved a tuning problem for keyboard instruments. Because of the nature of pitches, when certain intervals are perfectly in tune, others sound out of tune. For this reason, before the Baroque only a few tonalities were used. In equal temperament all the intervals are tuned slightly but equally less than perfect, so a piece can be written or performed in any key.

13. During the Baroque, keyboard instruments could not make gradual changes in dynamic levels. So the dynamics during this time were terraced, meaning they often changed abruptly from one level to another.

14. When keyboard players accompanied singers or other instruments, they often read a musical shorthand called figured bass. Figured bass consisted of numbers and accidentals (sharps, flats and natural signs) that told the keyboard player which chords to play. Playing music from figured bass is called realization.

15. The continuo (short for basso continuo) provides a steady, persistent rhythmic and harmonic foundation for the music. It sounds the basic notes of the chords usually in a continuous steady rhythm. The continuo part is played by the harpsichord and other low-pitched instruments such as the cello and bassoon.

Musical Terms

antiphonal; polychoral
recitative
equal temperament
continuo
improvisation

figured bass
doctrine of affections
terraced dynamics
tonal center; tonic key

Chapter 11 Review

Oratorio and Cantata

Main Points

1. An oratorio is a long work for chorus, soloists, and orchestra. It consists of recitatives, arias, and choruses, but has no scenery, costumes, or acting. Oratorios are usually on religious topics, especially Old Testament stories. Because they are long, they were not composed for worship services.

2. An aria is a vocal solo with much more instrumental accompaniment than a recitative. It is usually melodic. Arias are also longer than recitatives, with words and phrases repeated to create an emotional impact. They are often in ternary from (*ABA* or da capo form) or binary form (*AB*).

3. Many arias contain virtuoso passages that show off the soloist's singing skill.

4. Chorus parts are sung by a chorus. Often choruses feature imitation in which one part enters and then another part follows a little bit later singing the same melody. They are rather long and accompanied.

5. Both choruses and arias are strongly metrical.

6. A chorale is a Lutheran hymn. It has a strong, simple tune. Chorales are musically important because they became the basis of many other works of music, both vocal and instrumental.

7. A cantata is much shorter than an oratorio, and its was intended for performance during a worship service. It consists of recitatives, arias, and choruses. Usually cantatas feature a chorale melody in some of their sections.

8. A Passion is an oratorio based on the events of Good Friday.

Musical Terms

aria   chorus
oratorio   cantata
chorale   virtuoso
passion

Chapter 12 Review

Opera in the Baroque

<u>Main Points</u>

1. Opera was developed by a group of noblemen in Florence, Italy, who wanted to recapture the dramatic qualities in music that existed in ancient Greek dramas.

2. Because opera is a type of theater, it has certain conventions that listeners need to understand and accept in order to appreciate it:

- Nearly all the words are sung, not spoken
- The singing style must be powerful enough to project the words and music throughout the opera house or auditorium. This style of singing is unfamiliar to most people.
- The words are often in a language other than English, which makes them impossible for most Americans to understand unless they follow a translation.
- Opera dialogues must be shortened to keep them from being too long. Much more time is required to express a thought in music than to speak those same words. As a result, the realistic quality may sometimes suffer.
- Opera requires the suspension of the same realities that affect any drama. For example, large blocks of time are often supposed to have passed between changes of scene, and the viewers/listeners observe scenes as if a wall in front of them had been removed so they can see and hear what's taking place on stage, and so forth.

3. Opera can be enjoyed much more if you realize that its purpose is not to imitate reality, but rather to heighten it. It is not bound by logic. Instead, it appeals to the imagination through the power of music to project basic human emotions.

4. The text of an opera is called the libretto. It is written before the music, and is seldom written by the composer. In performance, the translation of the libretto often appears on a screen above the stage.

5. The music of an opera consists of recitatives, arias, and choruses. The chorus usually participates on stage from behind the main characters. The music often features a ground bass or ostinato (meaning "stubborn"); a persistently repeated musical phrase usually in the bass.

6. Several traditions exist about the type of voices and the characters portrayed. The heroine and hero are usually a soprano and a tenor; a villain or authority figure is often a bass.

Musical Terms

libretto   ostinato
ground bass   ensemble

Chapter 13 Review

Baroque Instrumental Music: Suite and Sonata

Main Points

1. Several orchestral instruments were important in Baroque music. The harpsichord played an important role in providing harmony in most instrumental works, in addition to its solo music. The flute was similar to the recorder instrument of today. Trumpets had no valves, and violin strings were made of different materials and the bows were slightly different.

2. Some works like Pachelbel's Canon in D used an ostinato (basso ostinato) or ground bass, similar to that in "Dido's Lament" by Purcell.

3. Suites of stylized dances were common. They could be for harpsichord alone or for a group of instruments.

4. The sonata first appeared in the Baroque and referred to an instrumental work for one or two instruments. The church sonata (*sonata da chiesa*) was serious while the chamber sonata (*sonata da camera*) consisted of dance movements.

5. The trio sonata was a favorite genre among several Baroque composers. It actually has four parts, two for the violins, one for cello, and another for continuo, which was played by a harpsichord and other bass instruments. The movements were often short and arranged to contrast slower with faster ones.

6. Instrumental music often uses generic titles like trio sonata and concerto. So it's usually identified also by an opus (meaning "work") number, abbreviated "Op." Until the nineteenth century opus numbers were not used consistently, so some composers' works have been catalogued by other people.

Musical Terms

suite   stylized dance music
sonata da chiesa; church sonata   Op. (opus)
sonata da camera; chamber sonata   canon
trio sonata

Chapter 14 Review

Baroque Instrumental Music: Concerto and Fugue

Main Points

1. The basic idea of a concerto in Baroque music is the contrast between groups of different size. The concerto grosso contrasts a small group with a larger one (*tutti*). Both groups generally play the same music.

2. Typically there are three movements in contrasting tempos: fast-slow-fast. The most common form of the movements is ritornello form, where the main theme

alternates with a contrasting section. A concerto grosso is usually performed without a conductor.

3. Program music is instrumental music that the composer associates with an idea or story. An early example is Vivaldi's *The Four Seasons.* But program music did not become popular until the nineteenth century.

4. A fugue is an instrumental work that presents a theme (subject) and a contrasting theme (countersubject) in imitation in several parts (voices). The subject and countersubject have different characters. Fugues are usually written for keyboard instruments, especially the organ, but are also found in works for orchestra.

5. Fugues generally follow this form:

	EXPOSITION				DEVELOPMENT	
Voice I	S	CS	FM		Return	Close
Voice II		S	CS	FM	and	with
Voice III			S	CS	development	subject
Voice IV				S	of	
					subject	
					and countersubject	

S = subject   CS = countersubject   FM = free contrapuntal material

6. Sequence is a musical technique that is used often in Baroque music. It occurs when a pattern of notes is repeated several times in succession, but each time at a different level of pitch, which may ascend or descend. Sequence allows the music to be somewhat different while also being somewhat the same.

7. Other types of keyboard music composed during the Baroque include chorale variations, chorale prelude, passacaglia, prelude, and toccata.

Musical Terms

program music
concerto grosso
    tutti
    ritornello form
fugue
    voice; subject; countersubject
    exposition; development section; episodes
sequence

prelude
chorale variations; chorale prelude
toccata
passacaglia

NOTABLE FEATURES OF BAROQUE MUSIC

- Dramatic, intense, grandiose style
- Expressive, recitative singing
- Quite a few virtuoso passages in vocal and instrumental music with decorative notes
- Regular metrical rhythm, except in recitatives
- Homophony and polyphony (counterpoint) both important
- Tonal harmony, with modulations
- Continuo part in many works
- Terraced dynamics
- Harpsichord and pipe organ important keyboard instruments; harpsichord favored as an accompanying instrument
- Two- and three-part forms; ritornello
- Oratorio, cantata, opera containing arias, recitatives, and choruses
- Concerto grosso, solo concerto, trio sonata, suite, and fugue

Discussion and Critical Thinking

1. In what ways do Baroque recitatives fulfill the Baroque desire for dramatic expression? Why is a recitative especially suitable for expressing feelings in music?

2. In what ways is a concerto grosso similar to a fugue? What characteristics of these forms are typically Baroque?

3. Why is it logical that opera developed during the Baroque period?

Part III Review Questions

These questions are a review of information and terminology using three different formats: matching, crossword puzzle, and multiple choice. The answers are found on pages 64 - 65.

Matching. Match each term with its correct definition by placing the appropriate letter in the space provided.

_____ 1. Continuo

_____ 2. Opus (Op.)

_____ 3. Concerto grosso

_____ 4. Libretto

_____ 5. Equal temperament

_____ 6. Fugue

_____ 7. Cantata

_____ 8. Suite

_____ 9. Terraced dynamics

_____ 10. Program music

_____ 11. Chorale

_____ 12. Ensemble

_____ 13. Sonata

_____ 14. Passion

_____ 15. Ostinato

_____ 16. Tutti

_____ 17. Patronage system

_____ 18. Canon

_____ 19. Oratorio

_____ 20. Sequence

_____ 21. Aria

_____ 22. Recitative

DEFINITIONS

A.   Sacred multisectional vocal work for church, often using a chorale

B.   An instrumental or vocal performing group

C.   A short, persistently repeated melodic, rhythmic, or harmonic pattern

D.   Solo recitation style of singing that covers the text expressively, similar to natural inflections of speech

E.   Continuous bass line for keyboard and other instruments

F.   A stately hymn of the German Lutheran Church

G.   System whereby a composer accepted exclusive employment under the auspices of a patron

H.   Term meaning "work," usually shown with a number to indicate the order in which the piece was written

I.   Levels of dynamics that change abruptly from one to another

J.   Large work for chorus, soloists, and orchestra, usually on a religious topic, performed without scenery, costumes or acting

K.   Multimovement instrumental work contrasting a small group with a large group

L.   Accompanied expressive solo song, often virtuosic, found in large vocal works

M.   Polyphonic composition in which the main theme (subject) is presented in imitation in several voices

N.   Instrumental works associated by the composer with nonmusical ideas

O.   Music in which one or more lines imitate each other for almost the entire work

P.   Technique of having the music represent the words being sung

Q.   Text of an opera

R.   Term meaning "all" indicating the larger group performs in a concerto

S.   A group of stylized dances

T.   Immediate repetition of melodic pattern on different notes

U.   An oratorio based on the suffering of Christ on Good Friday

V.   System of tuning in which all intervals are adjusted to divide the octave into twelve equal parts

Baroque

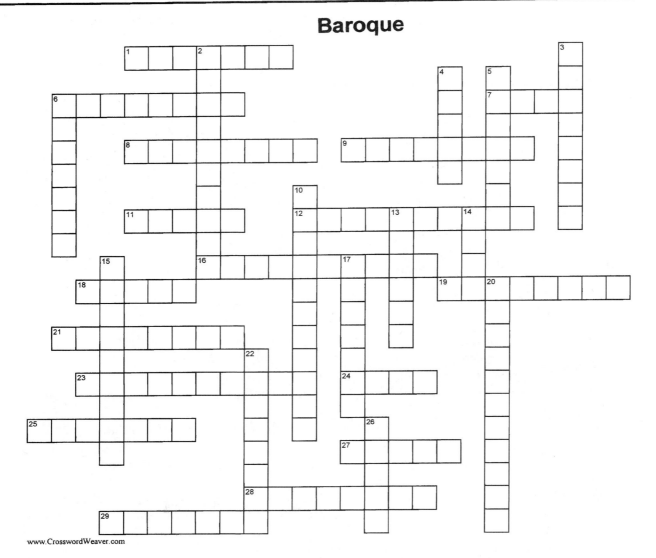

www.CrosswordWeaver.com

ACROSS

1 type of hymn in early Protestant churches
6 repetition of the same melodic pattern at different pitch levels
7 accompanied solo song
8 part played by keyboard and low instruments
9 a technically skilled performer
11 key ___ home key
12 this doctrine attempted to project states of feeling and ideas in music
16 opening section of a fugue
18 music in which one or more lines imitate each other throughout
19 short, repeated melodic, rhythmic or harmonic pattern
21 dynamics that change abruptly
23 group of performers that answer each other
24 a type of sonata for 4 players
25 type of instrumental music associated with nonmusical ideas
27 term meaning "all;" the larger group in a concerto grosso
28 text of an opera
29 short introductory instrumental work

DOWN

2 solo recitation style of singing that emphasizes the text
3 large work for chorus, soloists and orchestra usually on a religious topic   cantata   sacred multi-movement vocal work often using a chorale
4 polyphonic composition with subject presented in imitation in various voices
5 oratorio based on the suffering of Christ
6 main theme of a fugue
10 repeated set of variations based on a melodic ostinato
13 group of singers that sings choral music
14 work
15 system of exclusive employment with a noble family or the church
17 virtuosic work usually for keyboard
20 system of tuning
22 instrumental or vocal performing group
26 group of stylized dances

Multiple Choice. Circle the correct answer.

1. Three characteristics of the Baroque times are
    a. grandiose dimensions, balanced design, and love of drama
    b. love of drama, religious intensity, and interest in fantasy
    c. interest in fantasy, balanced design, and grandiose dimensions
    d. love of drama, balanced design, and interest in fantasy
    e. religious intensity, grandiose dimensions, and love of drama

2. The main goal of recitatives is to
    a. show off the singer's ability
    b. give maximum expression to the text
    c. demonstrate a beautiful melody
    d. inspire the audience
    e. tell a sad story

3. Which statement is <u>true</u> about madrigals?
    a. They were sung by men and women.
    b. They were sung at social events.
    c. They were sung in vernacular languages.
    d. They often use word painting.
    e. All of the above choices

4. An oratorio is made up of
    a. motets, recitatives, and arias
    b. madrigals, motets, and arias
    c. recitatives, arias, and choruses
    d. recitatives, interludes, and choruses
    e. madrigals, chants, and chorales

5. A chorale
    a. has a sturdy, simple melody
    b. has some of the characteristics of a recitative
    c. is used in Handel's *Messiah*
    d. was originally created to be sung by a chorus
    e. was originally written with four voice parts

6. A stylized dance is one that
    a. has been speeded up
    b. danced in the court of nobility
    c. is played only by professional musicians
    d. has been created to be listened to
    e. was composed to be played on the pipe organ

7. A Passion is
   a. a love scene in an opera
   b. an oratorio based on the suffering of Christ
   c. a love duet
   d. a type of morality play
   e. a cantata for soloist and orchestra

8. Equal temperament refers to
   a. a system of tuning keyboard instruments
   b. an even distribution of types of instruments in an orchestra
   c. the attitude of musicians who subscribe to the Doctrine of Affections
   d. the balance among recitatives, arias, and choruses in an oratorio
   e. an equal number of voices on each voice part

9. The main theme of a fugue is called the
   a. *A* theme
   b. principal theme
   c. subject
   d. countersubject
   e. topic

10. The group of four concerto grossi called *The Four Seasons* was composed by
    a. Vivaldi   b. Monteverdi   c. J.S. Bach   d. Handel   e. G. Gabrieli

Answers to Matching Review Questions

1.	E	7.	A	13.	P	19.	J
2.	H	8.	S	14.	U	20.	T
3.	K	9.	I	15.	C	21.	L
4.	Q	10.	N	16.	R	22.	D
5.	V	11.	F	17.	G		
6.	M	12.	B	18.	O		

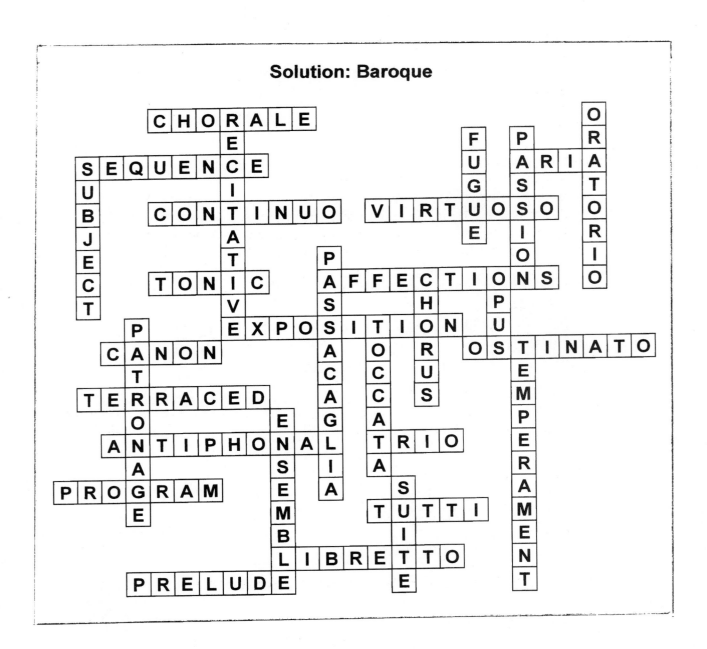

Solution: Baroque

Answers to Multiple Choice Questions

1 – E	6 – D
2 – B	7 – B
3 – E	8 – A
4 – C	9 – C
5 – A	10 – A

PART IV

CLASSICAL MUSIC

Classicism can be defined in two ways: as pertaining to the culture of the ancient Greeks and Romans, and as applied to the highest order of excellence in literature and art. The spirit of classicism implies that excellence has been attained in the past, and through adherence to tradition it can be attained again.

Like all stylistic periods, Classicism did not have a clearly defined beginning. The gradual transition from the Baroque to the Classical period began early in the eighteenth century with the Rococo or galant style.

Classical musicians thought of music more as a means of highly cultured entertainment rather than self-expression. This view encouraged the disciplined qualities of order, balance, symmetry, proportion, and restraint that have come to be associated with the classical style.

Historical Setting

The eighteenth century has often been referred to as the "Age of Reason" or the "Age of Enlightenment." It was a period of intellectual pursuit among educated people who greatly admired the artistic and intellectual accomplishments of the ancient Greeks. In fact, the word "classical" traditionally refers to the reason and restraint found in Athens during the time of Pericles about 400 B.C.

Admiration for the ancient Greeks can be seen in the art and architecture of the time. For example, many buildings used Greek columns and triangular pediments, including the Capitol in Washington, D.C. Paintings reveal a planned and balanced design and a certain staged quality and restraint.

Cultural life centered around major cities, especially Paris, Vienna, and London, as well as the palaces located in or near some of the smaller cities such as Salzburg in Austria and Mannheim in what is today southern Germany.

The nations of Europe, especially England, France, and Spain, struggled against each other to maintain colonies throughout the world. The Ottoman Empire, centered in what is today Turkey, was a world force that for awhile threatened cities as far west as Vienna. Democratic government was unknown at the beginning of the period, but before it ended democracies began to appear as a result of the revolutions in America and France.

Musicians and artists continued to work under the patronage system in which they accepted exclusive employment from a patron. This system worked great if the patron was interested in the arts; but the opposite was also true. The patronage system did not encourage innovation, because the purpose of an art work was to please the patron. Partly because the composer was considered a skilled employee, copyrights were unheard of, and composers freely borrowed themes from each other.

Intellectual Characteristics

The thinkers of this time adopted much of the idea-centered philosophy of Plato and Socrates in ancient Greece. It was built on several fundamental ideas:

1. *Truth through reasoning.* Scholars believed that reasoning and intellectual endeavor were the only means to determine truth. Emotions were considered a false approach. The intellectuals of the time were not impressed by the mystical or the unknown, because they believed that given enough time they could uncover truth through reason.

2. *Truth is universal and eternal.* Scholars also believed that the universe was governed by certain laws that cannot be changed. Therefore, what is true is true throughout the world, and it is true for all time.

3. *The natural order is right.* Jean Jacques Rousseau condemned the excesses of the government and civilization and praised the natural order of things. In America, Thomas Jefferson wrote a reasoned legal case against the King of England in the Declaration of Independence. In doing so he cited "the Laws of Nature and Nature's God." As statesman and scholar who was the third president of the United States, Jefferson could easily be considered the epitome of the intellectual person for the Age of Enlightenment.

4. *Fascination with science.* The belief in the universal and natural order of things encouraged a great interest in how the universe worked. Many learned people of the time were amateur scientists and inventors. Benjamin Franklin developed the Franklin stove, bifocal glasses, a musical instrument called the glass harmonica, and discovered electricity.

Musical Features

Melody -- pleasant and tuneful; singable. Melodies are often made up of short phrases (two or four measures long) in a statement-answer pattern. The music was mostly homophonic - melody plus accompaniment.

Rhythm -- steady and metrical, except for recitatives

Dynamics -- use of crescendo and decrescendo

Harmony -- becomes a backdrop and does not draw attention to itself. The tonal harmony of the Baroque continued, but the continuo part is abandoned, and chords change less frequently.

Timbre -- the orchestra consists basically of strings plus pairs of flutes, oboes, bassoons, French horns, trumpets, and later clarinets. The percussion section consists mostly of timpani. The piano replaces the harpsichord, but pianos did not have as powerful a sound as they do today.

Texture -- mostly homophonic texture, with occasional counterpoint

Forms -- several new and important forms are developed or perfected: sonata-allegro form, theme and variations, rondo, and minuet and trio. (Remember that these forms refer to individual movements, not genres.)

New Instrumental Genres -- symphony, string quartet, solo sonata for piano and other instruments, and solo concerto. Most genres are large works that contain several movements or independent sections.

Continued Important Genres -- opera and large choral works such as Masses and Requiems

Performance -- public concerts became available for the first time in larger cities. Orchestras grew in size but were quite small compared to those of today. They used only pairs of winds and brasses, had no trombones or tubas, and only one timpani for percussion. The level of performance was not high compared to today's standards.

Chapter 15 Review

Classicism and Classical Music

Main Points

1. The dates of the Classical period are approximately 1750-1820. Musically the center was Vienna, Austria.

2. Four persons stand out as intellectual leaders: Voltaire, Jean Jacques Rousseau, Benjamin Franklin, and Thomas Jefferson.

3. The admiration of the earlier Greek and Roman civilizations can be seen in the architecture, painting, music, and philosophy of the period.

4. The Rococo predated the Classical period. It was basically centered in France and reflected the attitudes of the aristocracy. The style was decorative, light, and ornate and was also known as the galant style.

5. The patronage system prevailed.

6. The development of instrumental forms and genres was a very important contribution of Classical composers. This is referred to as absolute music.

Musical Terms

Classicism
Rococo
galant style
patronage system
absolute music

Chapter 16 Review

Sonata Form

Main Points

The most important form developed during the Classical period was sonata form. It features the development of themes, and was used for the first movements of most symphonies and numerous multi-movement works for the next hundred or more years. Sonata form can be represented:

EXPOSITION					**DEVELOPMENT**	**RECAPITULATION**				
First theme (tonic)	Trans.	Second theme (dominant ....) (or relative major)	Trans.	Codetta	Working over of musical ideas. Rarely are new melodies introduced	First theme (tonic ....)	Trans.	Second theme	Trans.	Coda

Mozart's works were catalogued after his death by Ludwig Köchel and so are partly identified by the letter K. instead of opus numbers.

Musical Terms

sonata form
    exposition
    transition
    development
    recapitulation

codetta; coda
chromatic
K. (Köchel)

Listening Suggestions

Wolfgang Amadeus Mozart -- Symphony No. 40, first movement

- Listen carefully and try to remember at least the beginning of the first theme. Then notice what Mozart does with the theme in the development section.

- Notice that the transition between the first and second themes ends with two short chords followed by a rest. This helps to define the form.

LISTENERS' SCORE

Mozart: Symphony No. 40, first movement: CD1, 38

Chapter 17 Review

The Concerto

Main Points

1. The solo concerto was the main type of concerto written in the Classical period. A concerto features one soloist contrasted with an orchestra.

2. Concertos differed in the number of players and the difficulty of the music. The solo part was technically more difficult and more virtuosic.

3. Cadenzas are found in one or more movements, especially the first. Composers usually marked the places for cadenzas, but the performers were expected to improvise their own.

4. First movements of concertos are almost always in sonata form, but they have a double exposition - one for the orchestra and another for the soloist playing with the orchestra.

5. Rondo form had been around long before the Classical period. Originally it was a phrase of music repeated several times, but each time with different music in between. Classical composers expanded on this concept. At least five sections are required for a rondo: *ABACA*. Seven sections are quite common, especially *ABACABA* (which is sometimes called sonata-rondo). The main characteristic of a rondo is the return of the *A* theme in the original key.

6. Rondos usually have a bright, happy quality. They are often used as the final movement of symphonies and concertos.

7. The three movements of a typical Classical concerto follow this general plan:

Movement	Tempo	Form	Features
1	Allegro	Sonata	Double exposition Cadenza
2	Andate Adagio	*ABA* Theme and variations	Slow, melodious
3	Allegro Vivace	Rondo	Lively Cadenza

Musical Terms

solo concerto
double exposition
rondo

Listening Suggestions

Mozart -- Violin Concerto No.5, first movement
Franz Joseph Haydn -- Trumpet Concerto, third movement

- When listening to a concerto, notice how the solo instrument expands and elaborates on the themes.

- Compare the virtuosic solo part with that of the orchestra

- Notice how the themes are paraphrased in the cadenzas the soloists play.

- The third movement of the Haydn Trumpet Concerto is a rondo. Every time the theme returns it gives you the feeling of being back home again.

Chapter 18 Review

Classical Opera

Main Points

1. Although opera began as an attempt to revive the drama found in ancient Greece through recitatives, it soon evolved into a display of virtuoso singing.

2. Gluck began a reform of opera in which he tried to restore its dramatic integrity by having the music and the other components be an integral part of the drama.

3. Two types of operas were important during the Classical period: opera seria and opera buffa.

4. Opera seria was the traditional tragic opera that often featured stories about ancient Greek and Roman heros and gods.

5. Opera buffa (comic opera) was filled with frivolity. It was written in vernacular languages, and used humorous dialogue and sometimes included popular tunes.

6. Mozart composed both types of operas, with opera seria being in Italian and opera buffa in German.

7. Mozart's operas were different from Baroque operas. His characters were more human (rather than mythological or historical) and often made fun of the nobility. Because he was such a gifted composer, many of his arias and overtures (orchestral introductions) are performed apart from the operas themselves.

Musical Terms

opera seria
opera buffa
overture
libretto

Chapter 19 Review

Chamber Music

Main Points

1. Chamber music is music for small ensembles with one player on each part. Although more than one instrument of the same type may be used (two violins, for example), the music each instrument plays is different. During the Classical period chamber music was always instrumental music.

2. Chamber music was very important in the eighteenth century. Much music was required for performances in the palaces of the nobility, so the demand was great for music for small audiences. The Classical period is sometimes called the "Golden Age of Chamber Music."

3. At first, most chamber music was thought of as after-dinner entertainment. But as the century progressed, composers wrote serious and profound chamber works, especially string quartets.

4. If a string ensemble includes a non-string instrument, then the ensemble is referred to by the name of that instrument. So an ensemble for a violin, cello and piano is called a piano trio.

5. A sonata is a piece with three or four movements for piano alone or for piano and another instrument. It was an important genre of chamber music.

6. Theme and variations is an important type of music consisting of the theme and a number of different settings or variations of the same melody.

7. Minuet and trio is a three part (*ABA*) dance-like form in triple meter. It's often the third movement of four movement works.

Musical Terms

chamber music
ensemble
    piano trio
    string quartet
    woodwind quintet; brass quintet

sonata
theme and variations
minuet and trio

Chapter 20 Review

Piano Sonatas

Main Points

1. The piano became quite popular by the latter part of the eighteenth century and replaced the harpsichord. Composers wrote music for it using some of the same forms as for instrumental and chamber music. These works for solo piano, called "sonatas," are a vital part of the piano repertoire today.

2. The nature of piano music changed greatly from Mozart to Beethoven. This happened partly because of technical advances in the instrument, and partly because Beethoven thought of piano music on a much grander scale.

3. Many musical characteristics found in Beethoven's symphonies are also found in his piano music including many repeated notes, development of motives, sudden changes of character, use of *sforzando* (suddenly loud), and so on.

4. Beethoven's music is much more technically demanding than that of previous composers. He often uses the extreme registers of the piano. The pianist's hands must often move in contrary motion (opposite directions). His thirty-two piano sonatas are among the greatest ever written for piano.

5. In addition to symphonies and piano music, Beethoven wrote many outstanding overtures, chamber music, concertos, and vocal compositions. Some of his greatest works were written after he became totally deaf, including his famous Ninth Symphony ("choral") with its popular "Ode to Joy."

Musical Terms

piano sonata
contrary motion
sforzando
triplets
overture

Chapter 21 Review

The Symphony and Beethoven

Main Points

1. A symphony is a multi-movement work for orchestra that is usually divided into four independent movements. The character, tempo, and form of the movements is as follows:

Typical Classical Symphony

Movement	Tempo	Form	Features
1	Allegro	Sonata	development of themes; often dramatic
2	Andante Adagio	*ABA* Theme and variations	slow, melodious
3	Moderato	Minuet and trio	dance like; playful
4	Allegro Vivace	Rondo Sonata	lively often dramatic

2. Beethoven's music often contains much development of themes; he takes a short motive and works it over and over in different ways. The opening four notes (the motive) in the first movement of his Symphony No. 5 are probably the most famous four notes in all of music! (Even its rhythm is recognizable!) It appears often throughout the movement and provides a sense of unity to it. Sometimes it's inverted, and appears also in other movements as well.

3. Using themes from one movement in another was very rare when Beethoven did it in his Fifth Symphony. One example is the brief appearance of a theme from the third movement in that of the fourth.

4. Sometimes Beethoven will bridge one movement to the next without interruption, as the third movement merges with the fourth in his Fifth Symphony.

5. Beethoven loved sequence (repetition of the same melodic material on different pitch levels) and used it freely.

6. Beethoven greatly expanded the symphony. Among other things he often added a slow introduction, increased the size and importance of the coda section, and changed the third movement from a graceful minuet and trio to a lively scherzo. (The word "scherzo" means "a little joke" or "playfully.")

7. The third movement of the Fifth Symphony, which Beethoven called a scherzo, has many surprises. It seems like Beethoven is playing jokes on his listeners as the music suddenly changes character. In the Trio, a playful, rapidly moving melody is introduced by the low strings and then becomes a short fugue (fugato).

8. Beethoven's music contains many sudden and dramatic changes in character. Brusque, rough music can suddenly change to tender, lovely passages, and vice versa.

Musical Terms

symphony
scherzo
fugato
minuet and trio

NOTABLE FEATURES OF CLASSICAL MUSIC

- Balance, symmetry, good proportion
- Focus on form
- Absolute music
- Sonata form developed
- Chamber music was very important
- Opera was very important
- Development of opera buffa
- Symphony orchestra was established, although smaller than today
- Piano replaced the harpsichord
- Continuo was no longer used
- Tuneful melodies made up of short phrases
- Mostly homophonic texture
- Careful attention given to the use of tonalities

Discussion and Critical Thinking

1. In what ways does sonata form fit the intellectual emphasis of the Classical period especially well?

2. What elements of Beethoven's style are difficult to apply to vocal music? Could these characteristics partly explain why Beethoven was more successful as a composer of instrumental music?

3. Classical symphonies have four movements but concertos have only three. What reasons might have influenced Classical composers to omit the minuet and trio movement in their concertos?

Part IV Review Questions

These questions are a review of information, terminology, and listening skills using four different formats: matching, crossword puzzle, stylistic comparison, and multiple choice. The answers are found on pages 94 - 95.

Matching. Match each term with its correct definition by placing the appropriate letter in the space provided.

_____ 1. Rondo	_____ 12. Ensemble
_____ 2. Overture	_____ 13. Sonata
_____ 3. Symphony	_____ 14. Absolute music
_____ 4. Piano trio	_____ 15. Opera seria
_____ 5. Theme and variations	_____ 16. Chromatic
_____ 6. Scherzo	_____ 17. Patronage system
_____ 7. Chamber music	_____ 18. Galant style
_____ 8. Opera buffa	_____ 19. Coda
_____ 9. Minuet and trio	_____ 20. Sonata form
_____ 10. Sforzando	_____ 21. Double exposition
_____ 11. Fugato	_____ 22. K.

DEFINITIONS

A.   Music that is free of nonmusical associations

B.   Instrumental music for small ensemble; each part is usually played by one performer

C.   Chamber music written for an ensemble consisting of violin, cello, and piano

D.   Decorative light, ornate style prevalent in 18th-century French courts during the Rococo period

E.   An instrumental or vocal performing group; also the feeling of oneness in musical performance

F.   Form in which the theme appears three or more times with contrasting sections between: *ABACA; ABACABA*

G.   Melodic or harmonic movement by half steps

H.   A fugue like passage

I.   An instrumental introduction to a vocal work or an orchestral suite

J.   Mozart's works are partly identified by this

K.   Three part dance-like form in triple meter; often the third movement of four-movement works

L.   System whereby a composer accepted exclusive employment under the auspices of a patron

M.   An exposition found in a concerto for orchestra and soloist

N.   Italian term meaning a loud accented note or chord

O.   Multi-movement work for solo instrument, or for piano and another instrument, or for piano alone

P.   A large multi movement work for orchestra

Q.   The last part of a work or section usually giving the impression of an ending

R.   Italian comic opera

S.   A form consisting of an exposition, development, and recapitulation

T.   The third movement of some works, usually in a lively, playful style

U.   Dramatic opera, usually dealing with serious subject matter

V.   A work consisting of a theme and altered versions of that theme

Classical Music

ACROSS

2 Italian for "a little joke"
5 type of opera that is serious
6 suddenly loud with force
8 type of music for small ensemble
13 multi movement work for solo piano
15 type of quintet consisting of flute, oboe, clarinet, French horn and bassoon
16 form with an exposition, development and recapitulation
21 number of the movement in a multi movement work that is usually in sonata form
24 type of exposition found in a concerto
25 composer who became deaf
27 system of employment for many composers
28 number of Beethoven's choral symphony with "Ode to Joy"
29 number of notes in Beethoven's most famous motive
30 sometime called the "father of the symphony"
31 another name for ABACABA form
32 number of the movement in a multi movement work that is usually slow

DOWN

1 style of music during the 18th century French Rococo
3 melodic or harmonic movement by half steps
4 musical bridge between themes in sonata form
7 instrumental introduction to an opera
9 type of opera that is comic or lighthearted
10 music that is the opposite of program music
11 trio named after this instrument that also includes violin and cello
12 ending
14 a small performing group
17 and variations   work consisting of a theme and altered versions of it
18 multi movement work for orchestra
19 type of motion where the pianist's hands move in opposite directions
20 number of Beethoven's most famous symphony
22 like a fugue
23 child prodigy with a phenomenal memory
26 often paired with a minuet as the third movement of instrumental works

Listening Practice: Comparing Baroque and Classical Styles

Learning to hear the differences between works in different styles is an excellent way to improve your ability to perceive music. The first movements of "Spring" from Vivaldi's *The Four Seasons* and Mozart's Violin Concerto No. 5 are in two different styles. Listen to each of them. Then circle your answers.

	"Spring"-- *The Four Seasons* Vivaldi		Violin Concerto No. 5 Mozart	
Length	5 minutes	10 minutes	5 minutes	10 minutes
Major or minor key	major	minor	major	minor
Size of orchestra	quite small	not large	quite small	not large
Variety of instruments in orchestra	no wind instruments; some wind instruments		no wind instruments; some wind instruments	
Style of themes	short phases	flowing	short phrases	flowing
Number of themes	two	several	two	several
Theme development	very little	some	very little	some
Harmonies	functional	rich	functional	rich
Continuo	yes	no	yes	no
Form	ritornelli	sonata	ritornelli	sonata
Dynamics	somewhat terraced; gradual changes		somewhat terraced; gradual changes	
Rhythm	irregular	regular	irregular	regular
Texture	polyphonic	homophonic	polyphonic	homophonic

Multiple Choice. Circle the correct answer.

1. The Classical period occurred at about the same time as
    a. the first settlements in America
    b. the Revolutionary War
    c. the Civil War
    d. the Spanish-American War
    e. World War I

2. Which feature of Baroque music is not found in music of the Classical period?
    a. a steady beat
    b. major and minor keys
    c. basso continuo
    d. metrical rhythm
    e. large orchestras

3. The most important form used by composers during the Classical period was
    a. rondo form
    b. theme and variations
    c. minuet and trio
    d. sonata form
    e. binary form

4. The first large section in sonata form is called the
    a. exposition   b. development   c. introduction   d. recapitulation
    e. coda

5. Which statements are true about Mozart?
    a. became deaf later in life
    b. was a child prodigy
    c. had a phenomenal memory for music
    d. wrote more symphonies than any other composer
    e. composed mostly in major keys

6. Which is not usually found in a concerto?
    a. a cadenza
    b. a solo part that is more difficult and showy than the orchestral part
    c. a double exposition in sonata form
    d. a fourth movement
    e. a coda at the end of the first movement

7. Which statements are <u>true</u> about Haydn?
   a. wrote almost exclusively for the piano
   b. had an abusive father who tried to make him a child prodigy
   c. enjoyed a very good situation under the patronage system
   d. sometimes called the "Father of the Symphony"
   e. had three distinct periods of stylistic development

8. Which is a convention found in almost all operas?
   a. singers accompanied by guitar or a similar instrument
   b. most or all lines are sung, not spoken
   c. singers sing into microphones
   d. a chorus seated at the side of the stage comments on what is taking place on stage
   e. some audience participation, especially in the singing of well-known choruses

9. In Mozart's *Don Giovanni,* the statue that comes to dinner is
   a. Don Giovanni's father
   b. the father who died defending the honor of his daughter from Don Giovanni
   c. the image of Don Giovanni's own conscience
   d. Don Giovanni's brother who was a priest
   e. the ruler of Don Giovanni's country

10. A piano trio contains
    a. three pianos
    b. two violins and a piano
    c. two pianos and a violin
    d. a violin, flute, and piano
    e. a violin, cello, and piano

11. What is the main feature of a theme and variations?
    a. several variations are heard before the theme is played
    b. one theme is varied through changes in the melody, harmony, and so forth
    c. two or more themes are varied in alternating order
    d. a theme in three-part form
    e. the theme is usually a long, rather complicated melody

12. The tempos of the four movements of a symphony are usually in which order?
    a. allegro, adagio, moderato, and molto allegro
    b. adagio, moderato, allegro, and molto allegro
    c. molto allegro, adagio, allegro, and moderato
    d. allegro, moderato, adagio, and molto allegro
    e. allegro, molto allegro, adagio, and moderato

13. An important feature of Beethoven's music is
    a. dissonant harmonies
    b. many changes of meter
    c. much use of percussion instruments
    d. extensive development of motives and themes
    e. the prominent role of the harp

14. Beethoven's ideals are represented in his setting of Schiller's "Ode to Joy" in his
    a. opera *Fidelio*
    b. song cycle
    c. Symphony No. 9
    d. Symphony No. 5
    e. Piano Concerto No. 4

15. Which statement is true of the home keys of movements in a Classical symphony?
    a. All four movements are in the same key
    b. The second and third movement are not in the home key of the symphony
    c. The second movement is not in the home key of the symphony
    d. The third movement is not in the home key of the symphony
    e. The fourth movement is not in the home key of the symphony

16. An important improvement in the piano that occurred during Beethoven's lifetime was the
    a. addition of a fourth pedal
    b. enlargement of the keys themselves
    c. stronger frame that allowed for greater tension in the strings
    d. addition of a soundboard to amplify the vibrations of the strings
    e. addition of devices that allowed the keys to be coupled together

Answers to Matching Review Questions

1 - F	7 - B	13 - O	19 - Q
2 - I	8 - R	14 - A	20 - S
3 - P	9 - K	15 - U	21 - M
4 - C	10 - N	16 - G	22 - J
5 - V	11 - H	17 - L	
6 - T	12 - E	18 - D	

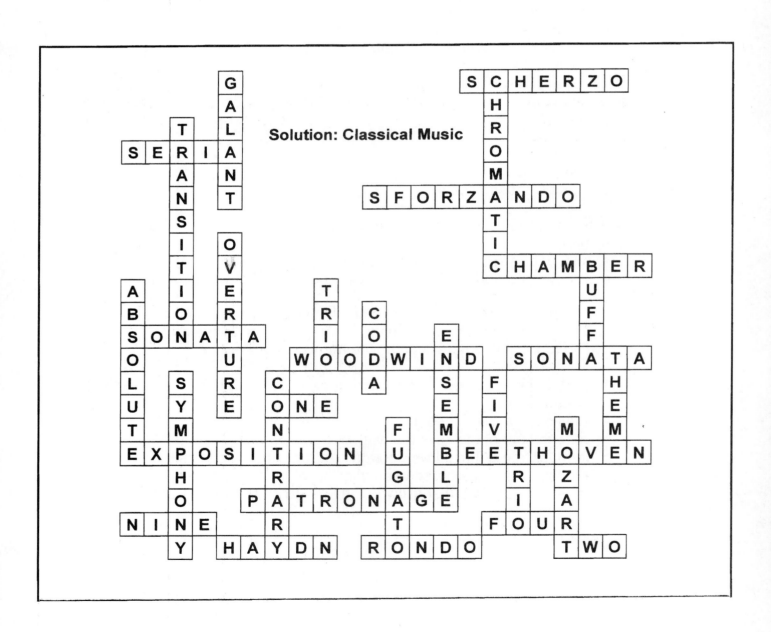

Solution: Classical Music

Answers to Listening Practice
Comparing Baroque and Classical Styles

- Vivaldi's "Spring" -- is about 5 minutes long, in major, uses a quite small orchestra that includes no wind instruments, uses several melodies with short phrases, has very little development of themes, has functional harmonies with a continuo, has ritornelli form, contains somewhat terraced dynamics, has regular meter, and is mostly homophonic.

- Mozart's Violin Concerto -- is about 10 minutes long, in major, uses a moderate size orchestra containing wind instruments, features two themes with short phrases, has some development of the themes, utilizes functional harmony but has no continuo part, is in sonata form, has many gradual changes of dynamic levels, regular meter, and is generally homophonic.

Answers to Multiple Choice Questions

1.	B	9.	B
2.	C	10.	E
3.	D	11.	B
4.	A	12.	A
5.	B, C, and E	13.	D
6.	D	14.	C
7.	C and D	15.	C
8.	B	16.	C

PART V

ROMANTIC MUSIC

The Romantic period covers almost all of the nineteenth century and extends into the twentieth, or roughly 1820 to 1910. Profound changes were taking place at every level of human existence. This was reflected in the art, music, and culture of the time.

Historical Setting

When the nineteenth century began, the nations of Germany and Italy as we know them today had not yet been formed. France under Napoleon Bonaparte had yet to conquer much of Europe, and then meet its end at Waterloo in 1814. During the remainder of the century Europe saw one broken treaty and war after another, including a war between France and Germany. It was a time of intense feelings of nationalism in the midst of political turmoil.

Dominance of the nobility was beginning to weaken. The industrial revolution increased the wealth and power of the emerging merchant-entrepreneur class. More and more concerts were given in public concert halls rather than private palaces. Several renowned performers like the violinist Niccolo Paganini and pianist Franz Liszt toured extensively and became musical idols of their day.

As a result of the industrial revolution, instruments were greatly improved. They became more affordable, and new ones were invented. Music could now be written that would have been unplayable in earlier centuries. Valves were added to trumpets, French horns, and tubas, and the woodwinds were given additional keys. Pedal mechanisms were developed for the harp and the timpani. Such technical improvements made it possible to play all the notes in the chromatic scale. The piano acquired a cast iron frame and thicker strings, which resulted in a stronger, more brilliant tone quality.

The gradual rise of democracy produced better educational opportunities. New conservatories were established to provide better training. Many symphony orchestras were founded and increased greatly in size. They performed throughout the major cities of Europe, and by the end of the century in America as well.

Musical Features

Melody -- Often flowing, warm, and passionate

Rhythm -- Generally metrical with regularly recurring beats. But often *rubato* is used in which slight rhythmic deviations are made for expressive purposes.

Dynamics -- Extreme ranges are used from very soft to very loud. Frequent changes between loud and soft; often a gradual, extended crescendo leads up to a climactic point.

Harmony -- Rich, full-sounding chords and many chromatic alterations. Later in the period the feeling of a tonal center is weakened because of altered chords and frequent modulations.

Timbre -- The size of the orchestra increases significantly, more instruments are doubled and new instruments added (bass clarinet, bass trombone, English horn, piccolo, harp). Composers become more skilled at bringing out the special qualities of each type of instrument (orchestration).

Texture -- Homophonic texture predominates

Forms - - Followed rather freely when used

New Types

- Virtuoso music
- Instrumental -- program music, character pieces
- Vocal genre -- art song

Continued Important Genres - - symphony, concerto, chamber music, opera, and choral works

Chapter 22 Review

Romance and Romanticism

Main Points

Romanticism was an artistic point of view that had these characteristics:

1. *Fascination with the unknown.* Romantic writers, artists, and musicians were impressed with the mystery of the world and the power of evil. The Faust legend about a man who sells his soul to the devil was a popular topic, as was the "Dies irae" theme from the Requiem Mass.

2. *Reliance on emotion and imagination.* Feeling replaced reason; truth became what was felt to be true. The poet Keats wrote in a letter, "I am certain of nothing but the holiness of the heart's affections and the truth of the imagination. What the imagination seizes as beauty must be truth."

3. *Fondness for the long ago and far away.* Romanticists considered medieval times heroic, as can be seen in the King Arthur legend and the fascination with the search for the Holy Grail.

4. *Attraction to the struggle with unknown forces.* Romantic stories, poems, and opera plots often reveal a struggle against overwhelming and magical forces, including curses and magic potions.

5. *Resentment of rules and restraints.* Romanticists felt perfectly capable of making their own rules; they cherished freedom.

6. *Fascination with nature.* Nature appealed to Romanticists because it represented the world untainted by humans. They extolled nature in songs and works of art, and they admired the simple peasant life, although they did not want to live that way.

7. *View of life was largely individualistic and often ego-centered.* Works of art and music became personal works that were a part of the creator's psyche. Some Romanticists were anti-social, while others sought the adulation of the public.

Musical Term

Romanticism

Chapter 23 Review

Early Romantic Music

Main Points

1. An art song is a musical setting of a poem for solo singer and piano. It originated in Germany and is often called a lied (song), or its plural lieder (songs).

2. The expression of the text is most important in an art song. It is a union of the text and music.

3. Art songs are almost never sung in translations because it is very difficult to match different words with the music effectively. This can make them hard for people who don't know the language to understand.

4. In an art song the piano does not just accompany the singer, but plays an equal part in telling the story, evoking the mood, or painting a picture.

5. Art songs are often performed in recital halls, which are much smaller than concert halls. Because only two performers are involved, and because art songs tend to be more subtle than operatic arias, a recital hall is a more suitable place for this type of performance.

6. Most art songs are through-composed, which allows the composer to follow the text without needing to deliberately repeat lines of music.

7. Franz Schubert, along with Beethoven, marked the beginning of the Romantic style in music. Schubert wrote over 600 art songs as well as numerous instrumental works. He died when he was just 31.

8. Women were discouraged from becoming professional musicians.

Musical Terms

art song; lied; lieder
through-composed

Chapter 24 Review

Romantic Piano Music

Main Points

1. The Romantic period is sometimes called the "Golden Age of the Piano." The popularity of the piano helped to shape the musical culture of the time. Not only were virtuoso performers drawn to the instrument, but amateurs were as well. The piano became the preferred instrument in the home and recital hall.

2. Almost every major composer during the nineteenth century wrote for piano.

3. In a day when there were no recordings, piano transcriptions (arrangements) were often the only way people heard musical works written for orchestra.

4. Numerous short, solo piano works were written that can be referred to as character pieces. They're sometimes descriptive and are usually intended to sound like the inspiration of the moment. Their various names include:

> Ballade -- songlike; name derived from ballad poems of the Middle Ages
> Berceuse -- songlike
> Étude -- "study" in French; shows off a particular playing technique
> Fantasie -- free-sounding, imaginative work
> Impromptu -- intended to sound spontaneous
> Nocturne -- tranquil and songlike; the word means "night song"
> Mazurka -- dance from Chopin's native Poland
> Polonaise -- stately processional dance; national dance of Poland
> Waltz -- graceful dance in triple meter

5. Romantic piano works tended to be either powerful and brilliant (especially those of Liszt) or intimate and sensitive (especially those of Chopin).

6. Pianists use the pedals to contribute to smooth, lyrical phrasing of the music and other artistic effects.

7. Tempo rubato (taking certain liberties with the time for artistic expression of the music) is especially important in performing works during the Romantic period.

8. Chopin wrote almost exclusively for the piano. He is considered the national composer of Poland.

9. Franz Liszt was a great piano virtuoso who wrote very difficult music. He and the violinist Paganini were musical legends and idols of their time.

Musical Terms

character piece   piano pedaling
rubato   piano transcription
nocturne   virtuoso
etude

Chapter 25 Review

Program and Ballet Music

Main Points

1. Program music is instrumental music that the composer associates with a nonmusical idea. Instrumental music cannot tell a story, but it can convey general impressions. The program is indicated in the title of the work, which is sometimes accompanied by a poem or other descriptive material.

2. For Romantic composers, the program became a means of organizing a musical work. It was an escape from the strict forms used so often during the Classical period. It was also a source of musical material that had hardly been tapped.

3. Four types of program music were composed:

- •   Concert overture -- an independent piece in one movement with programmatic associations. Example: Tchaikovsky's *Festival Overture "1812"*

- Incidental music -- written to be performed between acts in conjunction with a play or drama. Example: Grieg's music for Ibsen's play *Peer Gynt*

- Tone poem (also called symphonic poem) -- a large, one-movement orchestral work that develops a poetic idea, suggests a scene, or creates a mood. Example: R. Strauss' *Don Juan*

- Program symphony -- a multi-movement descriptive work built around a story or idea. Example: Berlioz's *Symphonie fantastique* with his recurring fixed idea (or *ideé fixe*)

4. Other composers especially noted for their program music include the following that you may someday encounter:

- Franz Liszt -- *Les Préludes* and *Mephisto Waltz*
- Richard Strauss -- *Till Eulenspiegels lustige Streiche* (Till Eulenspiegel's Merry Pranks), and *Death and Transfiguration*
- Modest Mussorgsky -- *Boris Godunov, Pictures at an Exhibition*
- Bedrich Smetana -- *Má Vlast* (My Fatherland)
- Jean Sibelius -- *Finlandia*

5. Ballet is an art form that combines body movement, costumes, scenery, and music in an artistic way. The combination of physical and emotional factors marks its distinctive power.

6. Classical ballet began in European courts about 300 years ago. In the court of Louis XIV everyone was required to study ballet. Its main goal was to achieve grace and courtliness, not artistic expression.

7. Dance movements (choreography) are usually created to go with a particular musical work. Composers sometimes arrange suites consisting of works from the full-length ballet for concert performance alone.

Musical Terms

Program music
  concert overture
  incidental music
  tone poem (symphonic poem)
  program symphony
classical ballet; modern dance

fixed Idea; ideé fixe
theme transformation
orchestration
choreographer; choreography

Chapter 26 Review

Romantic Opera

Main Points

1. Romantic opera can be divided into three nationalities: Italian, French, and German, each with their own distinctive style.

2. Italian opera featured beautiful melodic singing (bel canto) and realism (verismo). Its best known composers are Giuseppe Verdi and Giacomo Puccini.

3. Grand opera was very popular in France. It was serious, spectacular, ornate, and often based on historical events. Lighter, more comic forms of opera also existed; opera comique and lyric opera. French opera was not as distinctive as Italian or German opera.

4. German opera tended to be longer and more heavy than the others. It was begun by Carl Maria von Weber, but the giant of German opera was Richard Wagner.

5. Wagner built his plots on Nordic mythology and the history of the German people. He wrote the librettos himself which is unusual, and organized the staging. He had a special opera house built in Bayreuth solely for the performance of his operas.

6. Wagner called his operas music dramas. In them he attempted to integrate all aspects of opera (singing, text, orchestra, and staging) into a total dramatic art work.

7. Wagner associated characters and ideas with melodic motives, which he called leitmotives (leading motives). The orchestra could play a much more important role than ever before, because through the use of leitmotivs the story could continue even when the singers were not on stage. His most ambitious achievement was a cycle of four complete operas titled Der Ring des Nibelungen.

Musical Terms

    bel canto
    verismo
    music drama
    leitmotiv

Chapter 27 Review

Late Romantic Music

Main Points

1. Romantic composers often used the same forms as Classical composers. But the musical material they poured into those forms was very different.

2. Brahms was especially skilled at taking themes and working with them, which gave his music a perfect combination of something familiar and something new.

3. Brahms uses both diminution and augmentation. In diminution the theme is presented faster (often twice as fast as the original). In augmentation the theme is presented slower (often twice as slow as the original).

4. Although the Romantic style is noted for its big expansive works, much excellent chamber music was also composed like Dvořák's "American" String Quartet.

5. The fourth movement of Tchaikovsky's Fourth Symphony contrasts a fiery first theme with a tender, simple folk melody. The development section brings back the theme from the introduction to the first movement. His works are beautiful and passionate.

Musical Terms

diminution
augmentation
chaconne

Listener's Score

You can download a line score of the fourth movement of Brahms' Fourth Symphony after you login at http://academic.cengage.com.

Chapter 28 Review

Nationalism

Main Points

1. Nationalism refers to the deliberate, conscious attempt to create works of art that are characteristic of a particular country or region. It's a very important feature of music in the Romantic period.

2. Nationalism is achieved in music by the use of folk songs, dance rhythms, songs about a national hero or event, musical descriptions of a country, and so forth.

3. Part of the impetus for nationalism was the desire to break away from the prevailing German-Austrian style that had dominated music for many years. Nationalistic composers often wrote tempo markings and other directions in their native language instead of the traditional Italian.

4. Because of political reasons the development of Russian music had not been actively encouraged. Early in the nineteenth century the Russian Five, a group of five mostly self-taught musicians, wrote compositions to try to preserve their Russian musical heritage. The least technically skilled of the group was Mussorgsky, whose opera *Boris Godunov* is among the most famous in all of operatic literature. He used musical techniques well ahead of his time such as whole tone scales (scales containing only whole steps), and polymeters (various combinations of meters, for instance, two beat against three beat meter).

5. Nationalism did not become evident in Spain and the United States until the twentieth century.

6. A phase of Romanticism known as exoticism was attracted by the splendor and mystery of Eastern cultures.

7. One of the most famous series of tone poems is Má Vlast (My Country) by the Bohemian composer Bedřich Smetana, which is nationalistic and programmatic. The best known of the tone poems is *The Moldau*.

8. The following are prominent nationalistic composers and compositions:

Russia	Modest Mussorgsky -- *Boris Godunov; Night on Bald Mountain; Pictures at an Exhibition* Alexander Borodin -- *Prince Igor; In the Steppes of Central Asia* Nikolas Rimsky-Korsakov -- *Russian Easter Overture*
Bohemia	Bedřich Smetana -- *The Moldau* Antonin Dvořák -- *Slavonic Dances*
Norway	Edvard Grieg -- Piano Concerto; *Peer Gynt Suite*
Finland	Jean Sibelius -- several symphonies and *Finlandia*
Hungary	Franz Liszt: *Hungarian Rhapsodies* (many of these)
England	Edward Elgar -- *Enigma Variations; Pomp and Circumstance* Ralph Vaughan Williams -- *Fantasia on a Theme by Tallis; Fantasia on "Greensleeves;"* Symphony No. 2 ("London"); and many choral works
Italy	Guiseppe Verdi -- several operas became associated with Italian nationalism Ottorino Respighi -- *The Pines of Rome; The Fountains of Rome*
Spain	Isaac Albeniz, Enrique Granados, and Manuel de Falla

Musical Terms

nationalism	tone poem
exoticism	polymeter
whole tone scale	

Listeners' Score

You can download a simple line score of the "Coronation Scene" from Mussorgsky's *Boris Godunov* after you login at http://academic.cengage.com.

NOTABLE FEATURES OF ROMANTIC MUSIC

- Intense emotional expression
- Nationalistic music
- Program music
- Virtuoso "star" performers
- Public concert halls
- Piano became a very important instrument
- Sometimes called the "Golden Age of the Piano"
- Character pieces written for piano
- Long works became longer; short works often featured
- Forms followed rather freely when used
- Much drama and contrast in the music
- Rich harmonies and flowing melodies
- Full dynamic range
- Distinct nationalistic styles of opera
- Increased size of the orchestra

Discussion and Critical Thinking

1. What characteristics of the Romantic era encouraged greater emphasis on the individual personality? Did this trend encourage the writing of music that was distinctly individual?

2. Can instrumental music (not just patriotic songs) express nationalistic sentiments? If so, how can it do this in musical sounds?

3. If instrumental music cannot tell a specific story, why were some composers in the Romantic period attracted to program music? What challenges and opportunities does a program work offer a composer that a traditional symphony does not?

Part V Review Questions

These questions are a review of information, terminology and listening skills using four different formats: matching, crossword puzzle, stylistic comparison, and multiple choice. The answers are found on pages 116 - 117.

Matching. Match each term with its correct definition by placing the appropriate letter in the space provided.

_____ 1. Music drama

_____ 2. Augmentation

_____ 3. Art song; Lied

_____ 4. Rubato

_____ 5. Transcription

_____ 6. Theme transformation

_____ 7. Étude

_____ 8. Incidental music

_____ 9. Bel canto

_____ 10. Choreography

_____ 11. Idée fixe

_____ 12. Polymeter

_____ 13. Nocturne

_____ 14. Concert overture

_____ 15. Program symphony

_____ 16. Diminution

_____ 17. Leitmotiv

_____ 18. Through-composed

_____ 19. Whole tone scale

_____ 20. Tone poem

_____ 21. Nationalism

_____ 22. Character piece

DEFINITIONS

A.   The alteration of a theme that retains its characteristic melodic intervals and rhythmic patterns

B.   A lyrical 19th-century character piece for piano meaning night music

C.   A song that contains no repetition of lines of music

D.   "Beautiful singing" in Italian; a style of opera in the early 19th century that featured beautiful, virtuosic singing

E.   Wagner's term for his operas

F.   Melody presented in shorter note values, often twice as fast as the original

G.   A performer's slight deviations from a strict tempo

H.   Deliberate attempt to develop art works that are characteristic of a particular country or region

I.   An overture not associated with an opera or drama

J.   Music composed to be performed in conjunction with a drama

K.   "Fixed idea;" recurring theme used by Berlioz in his *Symphonie fantastique.*

L.   A scale built entirely of whole steps

M.   Motive or theme associated with a particular character or idea in Wagner's music dramas

N.   Musical setting of a text for solo singer and piano

O.   A short instrumental work involving some technical aspect of playing

P.   Various combinations of meter such as two beat against three beat meter

Q.   Melody presented in longer note values; often twice as slow as the original

R.   Large one movement orchestral work of program music that develops a poetic idea, suggests a scene, or creates a mood; associated with Romanticism

S.   An adaptation of a musical work for a different voice or instrument

T.   Artistically designed movements of dancers

U.   A short keyboard work expressing a mood or idea composed during the Romantic period

V.   Multi movement programmatic work for orchestra

Romantic Music

ACROSS

1 set of variations on a short theme
3 melody in longer note values; often twice as slow as the original
5 another name for music drama
6 slight deviations from strict tempo
9 Italian composer of numerous operas
10 music performed along with drama
12 two or more meters at the same time
14 composer of Symphonie fantastique
15 bel canto refers to this type of singing
17 process by which a theme is changed but retains characteristic melodic intervals and rhythmic patterns
19 attempt to develop art works characteristic of a particular country or region
22 adaptation of musical work for a different voice or instrument
23 known as poet of the piano
25 composed over 600 art songs
26 number of music dramas in Ring cycle

DOWN

1 artistically designed movements of dancers
2 short instrumental work involving technical aspects
4 type of "musical poem" for orchestra
7 melody in shorter note values; often twice as fast as the original
8 short keyboard pieces that express a mood or idea
11 type of overture not associated with opera or drama
13 "night piece" for piano
16 motive associated with character or idea in Wagner's music dramas
18 German composer of music dramas
20 manner in which a song is composed with no repetition of lines of music
21 Italian word describing type of operas
24 type of song for singer and piano

Listening Practice: Comparing Classical and Romantic Styles

   Learning to hear the differences between works in different styles is an excellent way to improve your ability to perceive music. The first movements of both Mozart's Symphony No. 40 and Brahms' Symphony No. 4 are in two different styles. Listen to each of them.   Circle your answer to each aspect of the music. The answers are provided on page 117.

	Symphony No. 40 Mozart		Symphony No. 4 Brahms	
Length	8 minutes	13 minutes	8 minutes	13 minutes
Major/minor	major	minor	major	minor
Wind instruments	pairs	complete family	pairs	complete family
Style of themes	short phrases	flowing	short phrases	flowing
Number of themes	two	three	two	three
Development of themes	quite a bit	much	quite a bit	much
Harmony	functional	rich	functional	rich
Sonata form	yes	no	yes	no
Parts of the form	often clear	blended	often clear	blended
Dynamics	*p-f*	*pp-ff*	*p-f*	*pp-ff*
Rhythm	regular	irregular	regular	irregular
Generally homophonic	yes	no	yes	no
Complexity	somewhat	quite	somewhat	quite

Multiple Choice. Circle the correct answer.

1. Romantic artists and writers were especially fascinated by
    a. ancient Greek architecture and drama
    b. African artifacts and folklore
    c. the long ago and far away
    d. mathematical ratios
    e. the predictions for the future of Nostredamus

2. Which of the following best describes Romanticism?
    a. absolute music
    b. strict adherence to form and balance of phrasing
    c. reason, restraint, logic, clarity
    d. intense patriotism, nationalism, and personal expression
    e. loyalty to nobility

3. Which type of music is <u>not</u> associated with Romanticism?
    a. art songs   b. program music   c. etudes   d. piano music   e. motets

4. An art song is
    a. a folk melody that has been incorporated into a symphony
    b. a song about a painting
    c. an arrangement of a folk song for piano or other instrument
    d. a musical setting of a poem
    e. a solo song sung by a chorus

5. Which of these is <u>not</u> a famous ballet by Tchaikovsky?
    a. Swan Lake b. Nutcracker c. Sleeping Beauty d. Beauty and the Beast

6. Which is <u>not</u> a character piece?
    a. fugue   b. etude   c. impromptu   d. fantasie   e. ballade

7. The composer most associated with virtuoso music for the piano is
    a. Chopin   b. Beethoven   c. Schubert   d. Paganini   e. Liszt

8. A tone poem or symphonic poem is
    a. a musical work performed as background for a poetry reading
    b. a type of character piece
    c. music composed to go with a play
    d. a one-movement program work for orchestra
    e. an orchestral arrangement of an art song

9. Theme transformation is
   a. a melodic fragment that is subjected to changes in rhythm, harmony, and other features
   b. another name for theme and variation
   c. writing a theme or melody for a different instrument or voice
   d. a theme from an absolute work of music that is used in a work of program music
   e. a theme that has been turned upside down so the intervals that originally descended now ascend, and so forth

10. The composer most noted for writing ballet music is
    a. Schubert   b. Mendelssohn   c. Clara Schumann   d. Tchaikovsky
    e. Berlioz

11. The main characters in Puccini's opera *La bohème* are
    a. Clara and Drosselmeyer   b. Mimi and Rodolfo
    c. Rigoletto and Gilda   d. Roberto and Maria
    e. Faust and Thais

12. A leitmotiv in a music drama by Wagner is
    a. a style of singing
    b. a melodic figure associated with a character or idea
    c. the libretto
    d. a magical curse
    e. the term for the leading tenor

13. In the "Immolation Scene" from Wagner's *Götterdämmerung*
    a. Brünnhilde and Siegfried are reuntied and ride off together
    b. Brünnhilde dies in Siegfried's arms
    c. Wotan orders Brünnhile out of his castle
    d. in the glow in the heavens Valhalla and the gods and heros are seen sitting together
    e. the final leitmotiv is "Redemption by love"

14. Diminution refers to
    a. a theme played softly
    b. a theme with its note values cut in half
    c. a theme with its note values doubled
    d. a theme played upside down, with ascending intervals now descending and so forth
    e. arranging a work for full orchestra for a small ensemble

15. Nationalism may be expressed in music by
    a. using native or folk music
    b. giving musical directions in the native language
    c. vocal music about a national hero
    d. program music depicting native scenes
    e. All of the above

16. The Russian Five included
    a. Tchaikovsky, Borodin, and Mussorgsky
    b. Grieg, Rimsky-Korsakov, and Borodin
    c. Rimsky-Korsakov, Mussorgsky, and Tchaikovsky
    d. Borodin, Rimsky-Korsakov, and Mussorgsky
    e. Glinka, Mussorgsky, and Borodin

17. Smetana's tone poem *The Moldau* is associated with a
    a. river   b. city   c. ship   d. mountain   e. lake

18. Rubato refers to
    a. sudden accents
    b. doubling the note values
    c. making a long crescendo
    d. taking slight liberties with the rhythm
    e. change of meter

19. Which composer was innovative in introducing the use of the whole tone scale?
    a. Brahms
    b. Smetana
    c. Mussorgsky
    d. Wagner
    e. Chopin

20. The Romantic period is sometimes called the "Golden Age of the ------"
    a. voice
    b. piano
    c. opera
    d. individual
    e. arts

Answers to Matching Review Questions

1 – E	6 - A	11 - K	16 – F	21 – H
2 – Q	7 - O	12 – P	17 – M	22 – U
3 – N	8 - J	13 – B	18 – C	
4 – G	9 - D	14 – I	19 – L	
5 – S	10 - T	15 – V	20 – R	

Solution: Romantic Music

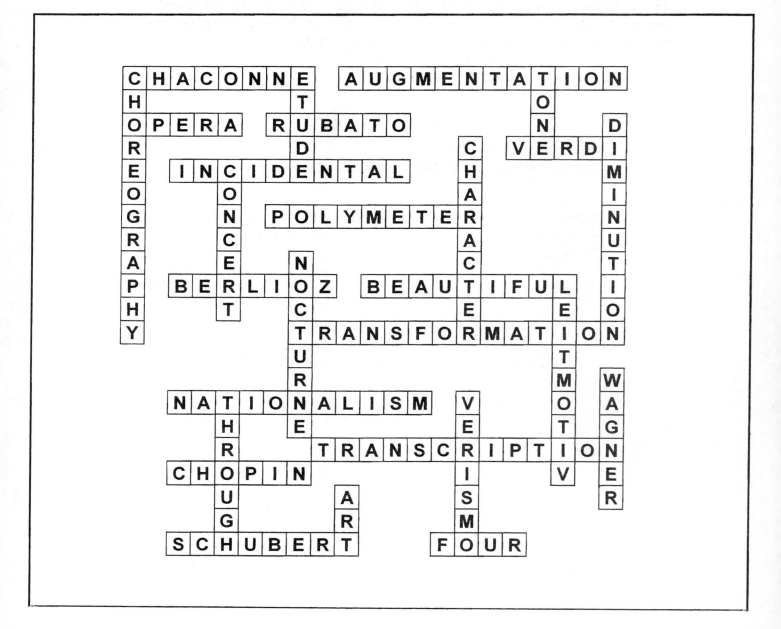

Answers to Listening Practice
Comparing Classical and Romantic Styles

- Mozart's Symphony -- 8 minutes long, in minor, pairs of wind instruments, short phrases, two themes, quite a bit of development, functional harmony, sonata form, parts of form are often quite clearly marked with cadences and rests, *p-f,* regular rhythm, generally homophonic, somewhat complex.

- Brahms' Symphony -- 13 minutes long, in minor, complete family of wind instruments, rich flowing themes, three themes, much development, rich harmony, sonata form, parts of the form are usually blended together, *pp-ff,* regular rhythm, generally homophonic, quite complex.

Answers to Multiple Choice Questions

1 – C	11 – B
2 – D	12 – B
3 – E	13 – D and E
4 – D	14 – B
5 – D	15 – E
6 – A	16 – D
7 – E	17 – A
8 – D	18 – D
9 – A	19 – C
10 – D	20 – B

PART VI

Twentieth-Century Music

The twentieth century underwent far more development and change than any previous century. These changes affected every area of life, including music.

Historical Setting

The twentieth century had the largest and bloodiest wars in history. Beginning with World War 1 (1914-18) and World War 11 (1939-45), plus numerous lesser wars in Korea, Vietnam, and elsewhere, armed conflicts marked most of the century. These wars often involved or resulted in massive political changes. Virtually everywhere kings were deposed, often only to be replaced by dictators. By the close of the century, however, democracies had replaced many of the dictators. The empires of England, France, and then Russia fell apart as one after another of their colonies or states became independent countries. Because of political divisions, the United Nations struggled to make even a small difference in world affairs.

Science and technology had a massive impact on this century in numerous ways:

1. *The nature of work.* Jobs that involved mostly physical labor gave way to machines. New jobs more suitable for women were created, often in the service area. Partly because of this many more women entered the workplace.

2. *Instant communication.* Technology vastly increased the contact with and knowledge of people everywhere in the world. Instant communication became possible with telephone, fax, and computer. Events from every part of the world can be shown on television as they happen. And any part of the globe is only hours away by plane.

3. *Higher standard of living.* Science and technology greatly improved the standard of living for most people, making modern conveniences more affordable.

4. *Music everywhere.* Music became an everyday commodity. Music that in previous centuries could be heard only by the privileged few now became available to nearly everyone.

5. *Longer and healthier lives.* Medical science greatly improved the quality and length of life. One result has been a large increase in the world's population, including an increased proportion of older persons.

Intellectual Characteristics

The events and developments of the twentieth century had a profound effect on its intellectual climate. A few of them are:

1. *Decreased optimism.* The optimism and confidence that pervaded much of the thinking of the nineteenth century became more difficult to find. Freud and other psychoanalysts brought out the dark side of human personality. The holocaust and other atrocities emphasized it. Cynicism became more prevalent.

2. *Existentialism.* The philosophy of existentialism (things just are and there are no deep meanings) was promoted in the writings of Satre and others.

3. *Communism.* The doctrine of communism became a reality early in the century. The movement engulfed Russia, China, and several other nations, and it had millions of followers throughout the world. By the end of the century it was withering, marked especially by the collapse of the Soviet Union.

4. *International awareness.* The peoples of the more developed nations (Europe, the United States, Japan) became much more world conscious. International trade increased enormously, marked by the development of international corporations. Cultural exchanges and cooperation also increased greatly. Artists and musicians became much more aware of the arts of other cultures, and often adapted ideas from them. Nationalism among the more mature nations dropped significantly, but remained very much alive in the new nations of Africa and Asia.

5. *Improved education.* Education became increasingly more important to societal and individual advancement. Reading and writing, the former staples of schooling, came to be only the beginning of an education for an effective citizen today in most societies.

6. *Status of women.* Women attained a much higher status during the twentieth century than ever before. Women became active in virtually all the professions, including government leadership, both in the United States and Europe.

7. *Respect for all persons.* This century promoted greater concern for and sensitivity toward the minorities, disadvantaged persons, and political dissidents. Human rights became part of the foreign policy of the United States and several other nations as well.

Chapter 29 Review

Impressionism and Post-Romanticism

Main Points

1. The basic outlook of Impressionism (1890-1920) was that experiences in life are based more on impressions rather than detailed observations. Impressionists believed that the arts should appeal to the senses, not the intellect. Therefore, delicate shadings of color were favored in both art and music.

2. Impressionism was centered in France. It's sometimes referred to as French nationalism because the nation was unified in its outlook.

3. Impressionistic music differs from music of the nineteenth century in a number of ways:

- use of whole tone scales
- smaller orchestras, often with no trombones and percussion
- more chamber music and solo piano works were written
- flexible, subtle rhythm with less feeling of a beat
- notes added to chords to create a desired color of sound
- parallel chord movement
- much less development of themes
- softer sounds, with delicate nuances of timbre and dynamics
- little use of traditional forms
- usually no deep messages in the music; just enjoyable

4. Post-Romanticism expanded on the Romantic outlook of the nineteenth century. Many works were larger and longer, and the music generally was very impressive.

5. The qualities to listen for in Post-Romantic music are the same as the Romantic music of Mendelssohn, Brahms, and others: beautiful flowing melodies and rich harmonies.

Musical Terms

Impressionism
Post-Romanticism

Chapter 30 Review

Music in the Twentieth Century

Musical Characteristics

Twentieth century music cannot easily be categorized into a few important stylistic trends. In fact, the term "new music" applies more to styles of music that developed throughout this century than to those of any other period.

Melody -- expanded far beyond traditional major/minor scales and flowing qualities. Use of modes, whole tone scales (built in whole steps), pentatonic scales (built on a five-note pattern), and chromaticism (half step progressions). Phrases often are no longer regular. Some melodies are barely singable; at times no melody is found.

Rhythm -- much more important than in previous centuries. Use of very complex, irregular metrical patterns, frequent changes of meter, polyrhythms (two or more different rhythmic patterns occurring simultaneously), and polymeters (two or more different meters occurring at the same time). Rhythmic ostinatos (short repeated rhythmic patterns) are also used.

Dynamics -- full range of dynamic levels from extremely soft to extremely loud.

Harmony -- expanded to include polytonality (the presence of two or more chords or tonalities at the same time). Chords are sometimes built in fourths and other intervals instead of the traditional thirds. Composers occasionally add notes to chords because they like the particular sound, not because the added notes affect the basic function of the chord. This creates more dissonance. At times, highly dissonant combinations of pitches are sounded together (tone clusters). The increased use of dissonance and altered (or chromatic) notes weaken the tonal center. Schoenberg and others developed a type of music that has no tonal center at all (atonality).

Timbre -- includes all types of sounds. Timbre is expanded through non-conventional production of sounds on instruments, use of all possible vocal sounds (shrieks, babbling, tongue clicks, and so on), and even the use of silence to create a musical atmosphere. Some musical works were developed around changes of timbre. Those for "prepared piano" called for items such as thumb tacks, rubber bands, coins, paper and other objects to be placed on the strings or within the piano's mechanism to create different timbres. The harpsichord and early musical ensembles increased in popularity. The palette of sounds was greatly expanded through electronic music, in which every conceivable quality of sound is possible.

Texture -- more counterpoint was written, and some of it is quite dissonant.

Forms -- all forms are possible, but a renewed interest in older forms developed, especially those used in Baroque music. At times no formal plan is discernable.

New genres -- electronic music was introduced; some of it consists of the manipulation of sounds recorded on tape (musique concrète), and some was created on electronic instruments and computer.

Continued important genres -- nearly all, but a special interest in chamber music.

Musical Terms

polyrhythm
polytonality
chromaticism
prepared piano
tone clusters

Chapter 31 Review

The Mainstream

Main Points

1. Many twentieth-century compositions were not experimental, avant garde, or allied with any particular approach to composing music. They represent the mainstream.

2. Some mainstream works were influenced by folk music. Others were influenced by musical practices found centuries earlier.

3. Bartók's Concerto for Orchestra is called a concerto because single instruments and sections of the orchestra are treated in a concerted way, like in Baroque music.

4. The Brazilian composer Heitor Villa-Lobos combines the styles of Brazilian folk music and J.S. Bach in the "Aria" from *Bachianas brasilerias*, which is a vocalise (wordless melody).

5. The English composer Benjamin Britten wrote for every medium and for varied levels of difficulty. He wanted his music to be playable and understood. His *War Requiem* was commissioned for the dedication of a new cathedral to replace one bombed out in WWII. He uses the text of the Dies irae but not the same music.

Musical Terms

folkloric
mainstream
vocalise

Chapter 32 Review

Expressionism and Primitivism

Main Points

1. Expressionism is an artistic viewpoint that features an inward, dark and pessimistic view of human nature. Schoenberg was the musical leader of this style, and Berg and Webern were his students. Expressionism was centered in Germany, and is the opposite of French Impressionism.

2. Expressionistic music is dissonant and uses sprechstimme, a vocal style that is a combination of singing. The best known Expressionistic opera is Berg's *Wozzeck*.

3. Primitivism refers to the artistic movement that was fascinated with the products of non-Western and nonliterate societies. The music often features strong and irregular rhythms.

4. Stravinsky's music for the ballet *The Rite of Spring* caused a riot to break out when it premierred in Paris in 1913. In addition to the subject matter and dress of the dancers, the music is quite dissonant and is often bitonal, meaning in two different keys at the same time. The rhythm patterns are irregular and forceful with many polyrhythms reminiscent of the wild beating of savage drums. While Stravinsky carefully planned everything, to those hearing the work for the first time it may sound like a jumble

Musical Terms

Expressionism
sprechstimme
Primitivism
bitonal

Chapter 33 Review

Neoclassicism and Tone Row Music

Main Points

1. Neoclassicism is an attempt by composers and artists to capture the spirit of the Classical period of the eighteenth century.

2. Neoclassical works of music feature:

    *   smaller groups, with an interest in chamber music
    *   shorter compositions
    *   use of classical forms
    *   a restrained, controlled quality
    *   frequent use of counterpoint
    *   themes composed of short melodic ideas that are connected
    *   more simple harmonies than 19th century works

3. Prokofiev's *Classical Symphony,* composed in the style of Mozart and Haydn, is one example of neoclassicism.

4. Tone row music was devised by Schoenberg in the early part of the twentieth century. It is based on the twelve pitches of the chromatic scale, which means that the music has no tonal center (atonal music). The row is not the actual melody of the music, but rather the framework around which the composition is built. It is also called dodecaphonic music from the Greek word meaning "twelve."

5. The tone row can appear in four different versions: the original row, in retrograde (backwards), inversion (upside down), and retrograde-inversion (backwards and upside down).

6. Serialism is the application of the principles of tone row music to other aspects such as dynamic levels, rhythmic values, and articulations (tonguing and slurring). It represents total control of the music. Webern, a pupil of Schoenberg, developed it after 1925.

7. Octave displacement, or using a note of the same letter name in a different octave, occurs frequently.

8. Klangfarbenmelodie is somewhat similar to pointillism in art. Various pitches of the melody are distributed among many instruments, just as little dots or points of color are used to create a painting.

Musical Terms

neoclassicism
tone row music
atonal
retrograde
inversion
retrograde-inversion
seralism
octave displacement
articulation
Klangfarbenmelodie

Chapter 34 Review

New Sounds and New Techniques

Main Points

1. Several composers extended Webern's serialism to cover most aspects of a musical work, or what is termed total serialism.

2. Chance (aleatory) music is partly or wholly the product of some chance event, such as rolling dice or dropping pages of the music on the floor. The American John Cage was a major promoter of this style. The epitome of his views was his work 4'33" which premiered in 1955. The pianist just sits at the piano for that long but never plays a note!

3. Musique concrète is the recording of sounds on tape, and then manipulating those sounds.

4. Electronic music is also produced through computers and synthesizers. Over the years this process has progressed from recording in analog form to recording in digital form.

5. Eclecticism is using what one considers the best elements of several different styles.

6. If human experience is a valid guide, it is clear that there will always be music in the future, and that the music of the future will be different from what it is today.

Musical Terms

    total serialism
    chance music; aleatory music
    musique concrète
    microtones; microtonal
    electicism

NOTABLE FEATURES OF TWENTIETH-CENTURY MUSIC

- Dissonant harmonies, polytonality, atonality
- Complex rhythm and irregular meters
- Melodies often not conceived in relation to the voice
- Nontraditional scales and modes
- Microtonal music
- All types of sounds included in musical compositions
- Renewed interest in counterpoint
- Renewed interest in music for small groups
- Expressionism
- Primitivism
- Mainstream music
- Experimental music; avant garde
- Tone row music
- Aleatory music
- Electronic music
- Folkloric music
- Increased importance of percussion instruments

Discussion and Critical Thinking

1. Sometimes composers today write music that is not beautiful in the traditional sense as people usually think of beauty in music. Why aren't composers content to write nice, traditional music? What does their searching for new types of music indicate about the outlook of composers in the twentieth century, as well as composers today? What does this outlook indicate for the future of music?

2. Should a piece of music be thought of first of all as a means for expressing feelings or as a sound object to be contemplated for its tonal and rhythmic patterns? Which approach do you prefer? Why?

Part VI Review Questions

These questions are a review of information, terminology and listening skills using three different formats: matching, stylistic comparison, and multiple choice. The answers are found on pages 137-138.

Matching. Match each term with its correct definition by placing the appropriate letter in the space provided.

_____ 1. Atonal

_____ 2. Polytonality

_____ 3. Primitivism

_____ 4. Mainstream

_____ 5. Expressionism

_____ 6. Eclecticism

_____ 7. Tone row music

_____ 8. Musique concrète

_____ 9. Retrograde

_____ 10. Articulation

_____ 11. Prepared piano

_____ 12. Neoclassicism

_____ 13. Folkloric

_____ 14. Sprechstimme

_____ 15. Vocalise

_____ 16. Inversion

_____ 17. Microtones

_____ 18. Serialism

_____ 19. Aleatory music

_____ 20. Octave displacement

DEFINITIONS

A.   Refers to tonguing, slurring, and the style in which notes are played

B.   A wordless vocal melody

C.   Dissonant music not in any key or tonality

D.   Using a note with the same letter name as a previous note but in another octave

E.   "New classicism;" works that attempt to emulate the techniques of those in the Classic period; sometimes called "Back to Bach"

F.   Music that is not experimental or committed to any one particular approach to composition; extension of earlier musical trends

G.   Musical intervals smaller than half steps

H.   Application of the principles of tone row music to elements such as dynamic levels and articulations

I.   A compositional technique that integrates several musical styles

J.   Natural sounds that are tape recorded and modified electronically

K.   Turning a melody upside down so an ascending interval descends and vice versa; rearranging the notes in a chord so its basic note is no longer on the bottom

L.   Two or more tonal centers sounding at the same time

M.   A piano with objects inserted to produce different timbres

N.   Twelve tone or dodecaphonic music; a piece based on a row of pitches that uses a special order of each of the twelve tones in an octave

O.   Music in which the sounds are partly or entirely the result of chance

P.   Early 20th-century style that emphasized subjective and often disturbing emotions; music was highly dissonant

Q.   The reverse version of a melody or tone row in which the first note becomes last, and so on

R.   Vocal style that is a combination of speaking and singing; associated with expressionism

S.   Music that contains rhythmic power and primitive expression

T.   A type of 20th-century music that contains folklike qualities

Listening Practice: Comparing Romantic and Twentieth-Century Music

Learning to hear the differences between works in different styles is an excellent way to improve your ability to perceive music. The "Waltz of the Flowers" from Tchaikovsky's *The Nutcracker* and the fourth movement of Bartók's Concerto for Orchestra are in two different styles. Circle your responses to each aspect of the music.

	"Waltz of the Flowers" Tchaikovsky		Concerto for Orchestra Bartók	
Major/minor/pentatonic	major partly pentatonic	minor	major partly pentatonic	minor
Size of orchestra	small	large	small	large
Style of first theme	short phrases flowing		short phrases flowing	
Repeatng of themes	some	much	some	much
Amount of dissonance	almost none some		almost none some	
Importance of timbres	somewhat	quite	somewhat	quite
Some satirical sounds	yes	no	yes	no
Basic form	ABA	ABACBA	ABA	ABACBA
Meter	regular	irregular	regular	irregular
Texture	polyphonic	homophonic	polyphonic	homophonic

Twentieth-Century Music

ACROSS

1 chance music
3 two or more tonal centers
5 music containing folk qualities
6 main body of 20th Century music
9 English composer who wrote for every medium
10 type of music associated with Webern
12 intervals smaller than a half step
15 composed Rite of Spring
16 turning a melody upside down
17 wordless vocal melody

DOWN

1 dissonant music not in any key or tonality
2 name for very dissonant combinations of tones
4 artistic view that emphasized overall impressions
7 reverse version of melody in a tone row
8 style of music that emphasized dissonance and disturbing emotions
11 famous symphony composed by Prokofiev in style of Mozart and Haydn
13 promoter of chance music
14 number of pitches in a tone row

Multiple Choice. Circle the correct answer.

1. Which is not an important "ism" in twentieth-century music?
    a. Neoclassicism   b. Primitivism   c. Serialism   d. Existentialism
    e. Expressionism

2. Rhythm in twentieth-century music contains
    a. regular metrical patterns
    b. polyrhythms
    c. ostinatos
    d. irregular metrical patterns
    e. All these choices

3. Twentieth-century music is characterized by
    a. long works
    b. mostly polyphonic music
    c. warm, beautiful melodies
    d. most vocal music
    e. increased levels of dissonance

4. Melodies in twentieth-century music are characterized by all of the following
    except
    a. a beautiful, singable series of pitches
    b. use of modes or nontraditional scale patterns
    c. many asymmetrical phrases
    d. a certain amount of cool, intellectual qualities
    e. a wider range and more awkward intervals

5. Harmony in twentieth-century music sometimes contains
    a. polylchords
    b. no tonal center
    c. chords built in fourths
    d. notes added to chords to create the sound the composer wants
    e. All these choices

6. A "prepared piano" is one that has
    a. been carefully tuned
    b. had tacks, coins, tape, etc. put in it to change its timbre
    c. had its pedals disconnected
    d. had its sounds electronically amplified
    e. a mechanism for playing chords by depressing only one key

7. Bartók's Concerto for Orchestra
   a. contains several Hungarian folk songs
   b. features cadenzas for several different instruments
   c. has four movements, one for each family of instruments
   d. features contrasts between groups of instruments
   e. has a satirical paraphrase of a theme by Stravinsky

8. Villa-Lobos *Bachianas brasilerias No. 5* is best classified as
   a. nationalistic   b. expressionistic   c. impressionistic
   d. neoclassical   e. folkloric

9. Which early twentieth-century style involved distorted images and the dark
   side of human nature?
   a. Neoclassicism   b. Expressionism   c. Impressionism   d. Exoticism
   e. Post-Romanticism

10. One of the features of Impressionistic music is the use of
    a. sonata form
    b. religious music
    c. chamber music
    d. subtle tonal colors and chords
    e. vibrant rhythms

11. Stravinsky's *Rite of Spring* is an example of a type of twentieth-century art
    and music that is
    a. romantic   b. neoclassical   c. anti-intellectual   d. nationalistic
    e. primitive and barbaric

12. Which is not a feature of Stravinsky's *The Rite of Spring?*
    a. irregular rhythm patterns
    b. dissonant harmonies
    c. interesting timbres
    d. theme and variations
    e. short melodies repeated many times

13. Neoclassical works are likely to contain
    a. traditional forms such as sonata form
    b. dissonant harmonies
    c. large ensembles
    d. long works
    e. virtuoso music

14. The main characteristic of a tone row is
    a. the appearance of the row as the melody of a work
    b. the use of the row as the basis for the work
    c. the appearance of the row in two different meters at the same time
    d. the use of all 12 pitches in the chromatic scale in the row
    e. the appearance of the row in two different keys at the same time

15. The retrograde-inversion of a tone row is
    a. one row upside down
    b. one row backwards
    c. one row upside down and backwards
    d. two rows sounded together, one upside down and the other backwards

16. When the principle of the tone row is applied to rhythm, timbres, and
    dynamic levels, it is called
    a. pandiatonicism   b. extensionism   c. serialism
    d. imitationism   e. eclecticism

17. Aleatory or chance music is music in which
    a. some or all of the combination of sounds are the product of chance
    b. unconventional instruments are used
    c. voices and instruments are always combined
    d. polytonality and polyrhythms occur at the same time
    e. there is no such thing as chance music

18. Musique concrète is
    a. music written according to a mathematical formula
    b. music made from the manipulation of recorded sounds
    c. music produced by a tone synthesizer
    d. an advanced type of serial music
    e. an another name for aleatory music

19. Perhaps the single most important musical development of the 1950s and
    early 60s was the emergence of
    a. aleatory music   b. dodecaphony   c. electronic music
    d. atonality   e. the prepared piano

20. An eclectic composer is one who
    a. favors electronic music
    b. holds a university teaching position
    c. uses what he or she considers the best of several styles
    d. sets trends for other composers
    e. favors electronic amplification of music

Answers to Matching Review Questions

1 – C	11 – M
2 – L	12 – E
3 – S	13 – T
4 – F	14 – R
5 – P	15 – B
6 – I	16 – K
7 – N	17 – G
8 – J	18 – H
9 – Q	19 – O
10 – A	20 – D

Answers to Listening Practice
Comparing Romantic and Twentieth-Century Styles

- Tchaikovsky's "Waltz" -- major; large orchestra, flowing theme, much repeating of themes, almost no dissonance, timbres somewhat important, no satirical sounds, *ABA* form, regular meter, homophonic texture.

- Bartók's Concerto -- partly pentatonic, large orchestra, theme contains short phrases, some repeating of themes, some dissonance, timbres are quite important, some satirical sounds, *ABACBA* form, irregular meter, generally homophonic.

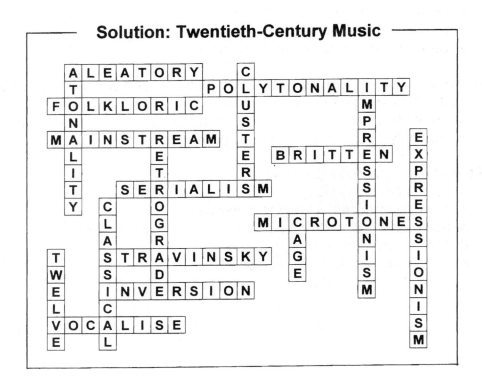

Solution: Twentieth-Century Music

Answers to Multiple Choice Questions

1 – D	11 – E
2 – E	12 – D
3 – E	13 – A
4 – A	14 – B
5 – E	15 – C
6 – B	16 – C
7 – D	17 – A
8 – E	18 – B
9 – B	19 – C
10 – D	20 – C

PART VII

Music in the United States

The United States has its own unique history and culture. Therefore, it has its own special blend of different types of music. American music in this Part refers to the music of North America, specifically within the United States.

Historical Setting

Although Native Americans had occupied the land for thousands of years, Western civilization began only in the early 1600s with settlements at Jamestown and Plymouth. And for at least a hundred years after that it was confined to areas along the Atlantic Ocean. At the time of the Revolutionary War (1776-81) there were less than four million people in America. Slavery was an accepted practice, and it continued into the nineteenth century.

The westward expansion consumed most of the nineteenth century. At first the settlements beyond the Allegheny Mountains were largely along rivers, which were the main means of transportation and commerce. With the railroads came the expansion across the plains to the west coast. The Civil War (1861-65) only slowed that expansion a little bit. Large numbers of immigrants came to America in the nineteenth century, mostly from northern Europe.

By 1900 the population had grown to about 100 million, most of whom lived in rural areas. The borders of the continental 48 states had been almost completely established, but Oklahoma and Arizona were still territories, not states. Waves of immigrants continued to come to America, but most of them in the early part of the century were from eastern and southern Europe.

Major changes took place during the twentieth century:

- America changed from a rural to an urban nation.

- Its population jumped to over 270 million, and many immigrants came from Asia and Latin America.

- Radio and television, as well as easy travel by air and interstate highways reduced regional differences among various sections of the nation.

- The United States became increasingly a world leader and involved economically with other nations around the world.

Intellectual Characteristics

For over a hundred years America's outlook and attitudes among educated persons were oriented toward Europe, especially England. After all, it had once been an English colony. The tradition of considering Europe as the source for the best in the arts and culture has a long history among Americans.

Because Americans were settling a new land, most of them had little time for or interest in the so-called finer things of life. A practical, pragmatic outlook prevailed throughout the nineteenth century and continued into the twentieth century, although it gradually weakened.

For much of America's history an optimistic "can do" attitude prevailed. American idealism and optimism, for example, were evident in President Woodrow Wilson's justification for involving the United States in World War 1: "To make the world safe for democracy." Such thinking changed with the Vietnam War and the many scandals that have plagued the national and state governments during the last three decades of the century.

The twentieth century saw a major change in the attitudes toward women and minorities. The rights and accomplishments of all people in all areas of life were recognized far more than ever before.

Chapter 35 Review

American Music before 1920

Main Points

1. The arts were slow to develop in America because:

    - the people were occupied with settling the new land
    - Puritans were suspicious of worldly pleasures, including the arts
    - there were almost no wealthy families to patronize the arts
    - Americans believed European music and art were superior

2. The most sophisticated music before the Revolutionary War came from the Moravian communities. The most notable American composer was Francis Hopkinson.

3. An early American composer whose works are still performed today was William Billings. He was a leather tanner by trade.

4. Most of America's patriotic songs consist of melodies that existed prior to patriotic words being set to them.

5. At the beginning of the nineteenth century, art music in the United States was largely undeveloped. Although several individuals made important contributions, much of its concert music was imported from Europe.

6. The piano music of Edward MacDowell is often performed. He composed an orchestral work that used elements of Native American music.

7. Band concerts were a vital part of the musical scene in the early years of the twentieth century. One of the most successful composers around the turn of the twentieth century was John Philip Sousa, often referred to as the "march king."

8. The most innovative American composer of the early twentieth century was Charles Ives, who actually predated some of the compositional techniques of European composers. He frequently quoted portions of familiar songs in his works, a technique known as "quotation music."

Musical Term

quotation music

Chapter 36 Review

Concert Music since 1920

Main Points

1. Following World War I American art music began to come of age.

2. A sizable amount of nationalistic American music was composed between 1930 and 1950. Composers consciously sought to promote American music by using folk songs and writing music about American places and events.

3. The composer most recognized for his nationalistic works is Aaron Copland. He was able to retain the interest and respect of trained musicians while writing music that pleased the general concert-going audience. He tried to bridge the gap between living composers and the general public.

4. Copland wrote a fanfare to recognize the common people rather than to honor royalty, which is usually associated with this type of piece. A fanfare is usually a short work for brass and sometimes percussion. While this composition is not featured in your text, you may likely encounter it in a performance.

5. As the century progressed, a number of American composers turned to the Neoclassical style.

6. Numerous musical trends came about in twentieth century music, most of which were reflected in American music. They include electronic music, avant garde compositions, Neo-Romanticism and minimalism.

7. Minimalism is a style of music in which the composer makes a minimum number of changes as the work progresses.

Musical Terms

minimalism
fanfare

Chapter 37 Review

Popular Music and Jazz to 1950

Main Points

1. Popular music is one index of the life and history of a nation. It's made widely known mostly through commercial enterprises.

2. The parlor song was an important type of popular music in the early nineteenth century. It was intended for home performance by amateurs.

3. The most successful composer of popular music in the nineteenth century was Stephen Foster.

4. Tin Pan Alley, the name for the popular music industry, became important beginning around 1880. These songs existed in sheet music form and were promoted by song pluggers.

5. Two important forerunners of jazz are blues and ragtime:

   - Blues -- features blue notes, which are the third, fifth, and seventh degrees of the scale lowered by one half step while the accompanying chords remain unchanged. The blues uses a 12-bar *aab* form.

   - Ragtime -- in two beats per measure with much syncopation (or "ragged" rhythm) and interesting rhythmic patterns.

6. Ragtime existed in sheet music and player piano rolls. These pieces were peppy and contained a lot of syncopation. By far the most famous composer of piano rags was Scott Joplin.

7. Blues moved from a type of folk music created by blacks to a popular genre.

8. Jazz is one of America's greatest contributions to the world of music. It grew out of several sources, but its African heritage is clearly the most important one. It developed early in the twentieth century in the brass bands of New Orleans. A number of elements make up traditional jazz:

- improvisation -- players improvise over the chord structure of a song according to certain guidelines
- syncopation
- melody contains blue notes
- performers make subtle rhythmic deviations
- distinctive tone colors, with instruments played with a jazz quality

9. As jazz emerged from the streets of New Orleans in the early part of the twentieth century, several types developed:

- Dixieland -- consists of two beats per measure and a busy quality created by several players improvising at the same time. It is usually played by a group of four to seven players, and was popular during the 1920s. Louis Armstrong became well-known as a Dixieland performer in the band of Joe "King" Oliver.

- Boogie-Woogie -- played on the piano, it features a familiar ostinato bass figure while the right hand improvised many decorative notes. It reached its height of popularity in the early 1930s. Fats Waller is associated with boogie-woogie.

- Swing -- created to be danced to and features a rhythm that swings. It is for bands of 12 to 19 players, and became popular during the "Big Band" era from 1935-1950. The bands played arrangements of popular songs as well. Duke Ellington and his band was a strong example of this type of jazz.

10. The person probably most responsible for popularizing early jazz was Louis Armstrong, who won over millions of people to this style. He introduced scat singing, a style of singing that puts syllables without literal meaning to an improvised vocal line. The most famous scat singer was Ella Fitzgerald.

Musical Terms

popular music
parlor song
Tin Pan Alley
ragtime
blues
blue notes

jazz
   dixieland, boogie-woogie, swing
break
scat singing

Chapter 38 Review

Popular Music since 1950

Main Points

1. Changes in American society have had a major impact on popular music.

2. Blues, rhythm-and-blues, and soul were developed by African Americans. Soul is a synthesis of blues, jazz, and gospel.

3. Country and variants of it were developed by whites in the South. Country music contains several influences of folk music. Its home is Nashville, Tennessee, and over the years it has become commercially very successful.

4. The musical characteristics of country music include:

   - A singing style that has a lonesome quality, with a slightly nasal clear tone and little vibrato
   - String instruments, including the fiddle, guitar, banjo, and mandolin
   - Melodies and harmonies that are simple and direct
   - Simple and clear rhythm, with only occasional syncopation
   - Lyrics that blend realism and sentimentality; the favorite topic is broken love

5. Several types of country music developed:

   Bluegrass -- retained country music's traditional quality by using no electric instruments or commercial lyrics. Its development was chiefly due to one person, Bill Monroe.

   Rockabilly -- a combination of rock and hillbilly (an early name for country music). Elvis Presley is the best-known performer of this type, although he is far better known as an early rock star.

   Country-Western -- also known as "Tex-Mex," it combines country with a traditional cowboy singing style. Roy Rogers, Tex Ritter, and Linda Ronstadt were some of its leading performers.

6. Rock contains elements of both blues and country music, but it also has strong social-political character. Its musical features include:

- Strong beat with a strong offbeat or "backbeat" -- 1 **2** 3 **4**
- Melodies and harmonies often contain folk qualities
- Tonal qualities depend on the particular rock style, for example, hard rock is loud with distorted sounds and a singing style that is often raucous and almost shouted
- Form is usually built around the lyrics, often of irregular length
- Stunning visual and dramatic effects are often used at concerts

7. Some of the various types of rock music include:

Rock 'n roll -- the early name for rock, which was given its name by a Cleveland disc jockey in the early 1960s. It features a "funky" sound, and was best-known in the music of Bill Haley and the Comets and Jerry Lee Lewis.

Soft rock -- appeared in the 1960s in the music of Bobby Darin and Neil Sedaka

British influence -- The Rolling Stones and The Beatles were very influential and popular from the middle of the 1960s forward. For awhile it was almost impossible to distinguish between the rock music of England and America.

Folk rock -- A type of rock strongly influenced by folk music. Its chief proponents were Bob Dylan and Judy Collins.

Acid rock -- A San Francisco style played at extremely loud dynamic levels and focused on drugs. Jefferson Airplane (later Jefferson Starship) and the Grateful Dead are two groups associated with acid rock.

Fusion -- A combination of rock with other types of music, especially jazz. Chicago, and Blood, Sweat and Tears were the best known groups of this type. Some fusion with art music was created by Emerson, Lake and Palmer.

Satirical -- A type of rock that poked fun at everything, including itself. Frank Zappa and the Mother of Invention engaged in theatrics and put-ons to entertain audiences.

Punk -- Rock that expressed a message of revolution. The Sex Pistols and Twisted Sister were two of its prominent groups.

8. Music videos were originally developed to promote recordings, but also have become a type of popular music.

9.   Jazz became much more sophisticated, much more of a listener's type of music. Several new styles developed:

> Bop -- originally called bebop; it contains nearly continuous syncopation, dissonant chords, and freely developed melodies. It's played by small combos. Primarily the creation of Dizzy Gillespie, it became popular after 1945.

> Cool jazz -- more intellectual and often contains counterpoint. Dave Brubeck and the Modern Jazz Quartet are especially associated with this type of jazz, which was most often heard in the 1960s and 1970s.

> Free form jazz -- involves collective improvising, no predetermined chords, and deliberate out of tune playing. It appeared after 1960 in the music of John Coltrane and others.

10. Popular music consists of much more than rhythm-and-blues, country, and rock. Some other styles include:

> Latin American -- first introduced as dance music -- tango, samba, and so forth. A type called "salsa" (meaning "hot" or "spicy") originated in Cuban nightclubs in the 1940s. Two well-known Latin American performers are Tito Puente and Gloria Estefan.

> Reggae -- Jamaican style with offbeat rhythm and chantlike vocal lines; texts reflected the beliefs of a Christian religious movement. Bob Marely and the Wailers were its main proponents.

> Rap -- features rhythmic singsong patter over a rock rhythmic background. Associated with African American music; often the words are street slang and express messages of protest and violence. Two of its main proponents, Tupac Shakur and The Notorious B.I.G., were murdered around the age of 25.

> Hip-hop – type of Rhythm and Blues that emphasizes the beat. Some of its groups are named after streets or neighborhoods and reflect the gang culture.

> Contemporary Christian – moved beyond its roots to become a segment of the music industry

Musical Terms

rhythm-and-blues
soul
rap
country music
fiddle
rockabilly
honky-tonk
bluegrass
bebop
rock
folk rock
fusion rock
punk rock; satire rock
Latin American
salsa
Tex-Mex
reggae
free jazz
Christian

Chapter 39 Review

Music for Stage and Film

Main Points

1. Music for the stage and film is created to contribute to a dramatic situation, although some of it is of a quality that can stand alone.

2. An early form of stage entertainment was the minstrel show. It contained songs, dances, jokes, and skits by whites portraying blacks. Vaudeville was another type of stage entertainment. It contained a variety of acts, and was supplanted by motion pictures.

3. Operettas and then musical comedies usually consisted of fanciful stories with beautiful songs, although some later musicals were quite serious. A few recent musicals are virtually operas.

4. Opera has not caught on in America to the extent that it has in Europe, although many excellent operas have been composed by Americans.

5. Music adds to the impact of a film in a number ways, including creating an atmosphere, giving clues about unspoken thoughts, providing continuity, and providing background.

Musical Terms

minstrel show
vaudeville
musicals
operetta; musical comedy

Two Listening Guides

Following are two Listening Guides for works that were unavailable for the CDs that come with *Music Listening Today*.

In the final scene of *Les Misérables* Cosette and Maurius locate the aged and frail Valjean. The scene begins with Cosette, Maurius, and Valjean toward the front of the stage. Fantine and the revolutionaries appear behind them as spirits when the light is focused on them. *Les Misérables* closes with the ensemble singing the marching song of the revolutionaries. The times in the Listening Guide are approximate.

LISTENING GUIDE

Schonberg: Finale from *Les Misérables*

(Valjean is seated with a blanket around him when Cosette and Maurius enter.)

0:00	Valjean:	Now you are here Again beside me. Now I die in peace, For now my life is blessed --
	Cosette:	You will live, Papa, you're going to live. It's too soon, too soon to say goodbye!
0:40	Valjean:	Yes, Cossette, forbid me now to die. I'll obey. I will try.

(Valjean hands Cosette papers on which he has written his life story.)

On this page
I write my last confession.
Read it well
When at last I am sleeping.
It's a story
Of those who always loved you.
Your mother gave her life for you,
Then gave you to my keeping.

(The spirits of the departed appear behind Cosette and Valjean.)

1:22	Fantine:	Come with me Where chains will never bind you. All your grief At last, at last behind you. Lord in Heaven, Look down on him in mercy.
	Valjean:	Forgive me all my tresspasses And take me to your glory.
	Fantine and Eponine	Take my hand And lead me to salvation. Take my love, For love is everlasting.
	Valjean, Fantine, and Eponine	And remember The truth that once was spoken: To love another person Is to see the face of God!

(The chorus of the departed revolutionaries appears at the back of the stage.)

2:25	Chorus:	Do you hear the people sing, Lost in the valley of the night? It is the music of a people Who are climbing to the light.
		For the wretched of the earth There is a flame that never dies. Even the darkest night will end And the sun will rise.
		They will live again in freedom In the garden of the Lord. They will walk behind the plowshare, They will put away the sword. The chain will be broken And all men will have their reward!
3:28		Will you join in our crusade? Who will be strong and stand with me? Somewhere beyond the barricade Is there a world you long to see? Do you hear the people sing, Say, do you hear the distant drums? It is the future that they bring When tomorrow comes!

> Will you join in our crusade?
> Who will be strong and stand with me?
> Somewhere beyond the barricade
> Is there a world you long to see?
>
> Do you hear the distant drums?
> It is the future that they bring
> When tomorrow comes!
> Tomorrow comes!
> Tomorrow comes!

4:08   The curtain falls as the music concludes.

The song "I Still Believe" from *Miss Saigon* is staged with Ellen and Chris in bed in America at a second story level and Kim at stage level in her tiny room in Vietnam. Chris has been tossing and turning in his sleep, and he has again mumbled a word. Ellen sings sadly to the sleeping Chris, "It hurts me more than I can bear, knowing part of you I'll never share, never know." Kim is still confident that Chris will return, because she knows that they have a young son. The spotlight moves back and forth between the two women as each sings about her feelings. The timings are approximate.

LISTENING GUIDE

Schonberg: "I Still Believe" from *Miss Saigon*

0:00   The song opens quietly with an introduction played by the strings and the harp.

0:19   At stage level Kim sings:

> Last night I watched him sleeping
> My body pressed to him,
> And then he started speaking.
> The name I heard him speak . . . was Kim.
> Yes, I know that this was years ago,
> But when moonlight fills my room, I know
> You are here ... still.

0:57   Kim continues:

> I still, I still believe
> You will return.
> I know you will.
> My heart against all odds holds still.
> Yes, still, I still believe.
> I know as long
> As I can keep believing, I'll live,
> I'll live.
> Love cannot die,
> You will return. You will return,
> And I
> alone know why.

2:04   Ellen sings to her sleeping husband the same melody that Kim just sang:

> Last night I watched you sleeping,
> Once more the nightmare came.
> I heard you cry out something
> A word that sounded like ... a name.
> And it hurts me more than I can bear,
> Knowing part of you I'll never share,
> Never know.

2:41   Ellen continues:

> But still
> I still believe.
> The time will come
> When nothing keeps us apart.
> My heart
> Forever more
> Holds still.
> It's all over. I'm here.
> There is nothing to fear.
> Chris, what's haunting you?
> I need you, too.

3:29   Kim and Ellen sing a duet, with Kim singing the melody and Ellen adding a
        contrasting part.

Kim:	Ellen:
For still	I will hold you all night.
	I will make it alright.
I still believe.	

As long as I

Can keep believing,

I'll live,
I'll live.
You will return.

And I know why
I'm yours,   For life,
Until we die.

You are safe with me.

And I wish you could tell,
What you don't
Want to tell.

What your hell must be.

You can sleep now.
You can cry now.
I'm your wife now.

Until we die.

4:29   The singers sing their long final notes on the word "die," and the orchestra concludes the song with a big crescendo.

NOTABLE FEATURES OF AMERICAN MUSIC

- Remained in the shadow of European music until the twentieth century
- Nationalism became evident in the 1930s to the 1950s
- Is strongly influenced by African American music
- Styles include neoclassicism, neo-Romanticism, and minimalism
- Popular music has paralleled the changes in American society including colonial broadsides, 19th century parlor songs, turn of the century piano rags, big band arrangements of jazz, country, rock, and pop
- Broadway musicals, musical comedies and film music in conjunction with technology have become very popular
- DVDs, ipods, computers and emerging technology opened up intriguing possibilities for music

Discussion and Critical Thinking

1. Suppose that you were commissioned to compose a musical work that would in some way be identified as American. What ideas would you consider? How do you think composers like Copland and Gershwin, for example, work American qualities into their music?

2. In what respects is jazz like concert music? In what way does it differ? Why do you think it evolved toward a type of concert music and became more sophisticated?

3. Which type of popular music do you think will predominate in the future? Will concert and popular music move closer together? Will there still be music of and for particular segments of American society? What reasons can you offer for your prediction?

Part VII Review Questions

These questions are a review of information and terminology using three different formats: matching, crossword puzzle, and multiple choice. The answers are found on pages 161 - 162.

Matching. Match each term with its correct definition by placing the appropriate letter in the space provided.

_____	1. Musicals	_____	11. Rap
_____	2. Scat singing	_____	12. Minstrel show
_____	3. Jazz	_____	13. Fiddle
_____	4. Swing	_____	14. Vaudeville
_____	5. Ragtime	_____	15. Break
_____	6. Quotation music	_____	16. Tin Pan Alley
_____	7. Minimalism	_____	17. Parlor song
_____	8. Operetta	_____	18. Soul
_____	9. Blues	_____	19. Bluegrass
_____	10. Blue notes	_____	20. Dixieland

DEFINITIONS

A.   Notes that are bent or lowered slightly in pitch, especially the 3rd, 5th, and 7th tones; common in blues and jazz

B.   African American style of music developed in 20th century America characterized by improvisation and syncopated rhythms

C.   Jazz style of singing that sets syllables to an improvised vocal line

D.   Type of musical theater that combines music, acting, staging, and dancing

E.   Type of popular music arranged for big bands, containing many jazz influences

F.   A forerunner of jazz, usually for piano in a marchlike style with a syncopated melody

G.   Light opera with fanciful stories and beautiful songs

H.   20th century style that features the repetition of musical patterns with a minimum amount of change

I.   Type of solo song associated with African Americans that refers to the form and style of singing

J.   Music that makes extensive use of quotations from other music

K.   General term for several types of African American music

L.   Jazz style for a small group of players in duple meter and lively tempo

M.   Type of African American music that consists of rapid delivery of words in a singsong style

N.   Name associated with the popular music industry

O.   Sentimental type of song popular in the nineteenth century

P.   Popular form of entertainment consisting of four actor/performers and a variety of light-hearted acts

Q.   Contrasting section in the trio of a march; sometimes called "dogfight"

R.   Violin modified for country music

S.   Type of country music that uses acoustic instruments to better capture its original qualities

T.   Popular type of stage entertainment in the early twentieth century consisting of music and other variety acts

Music in the U.S.

ACROSS

1 musical theater that combines music, acting, staging, and dancing

5 type of music containing folk like qualities especially popular with white culture of the American South

8 country music that uses acoustic instruments to capture original qualities

10 advanced jazz style for small group with much syncopation and flowing melodic line

12 violin modified for country music

16 early American stage works that preceded musical comedies

17 African American 20th century music with improvisation and syncopated rhythms

18 popular type of stage entertainment with music and variety acts

19 type of music in which a minimum of changes occur

20 also called "dogfight"

21 type of show with four performers and a variety of light-hearted acts

DOWN

2 big band music containing many jazz influences

3 general term for several types of African American music

4 notes that are bent or lowered slightly in pitch

6 forerunner of jazz, usually for piano in a march like style and syncopated melody

7 home of the Grand Ole Opry house; also called "Music City, USA"

9 jazz style of improvised singing using syllables

10 solo song associated with African Americans that refers to the form and style of singing

11 type of music that uses quotations from other music

12 short work for brass and percussion, usually associated with royalty

13 jazz style for a small group of players in duple meter and lively tempo

14 African American music using rapid delivery of words in a singsong style

15 type of sentimental song popular in the nineteenth century

Multiple Choice. Circle the correct answer.

1. American music had a slow start because
    a. musicians were persecuted in the colonies
    b. survival was the most important concern
    c. the Puritans thought that art and theater were wicked
    d. music was considered much less important than art
    e. choices B and C

2. Who was an important early American composer?
    a. Lowell Mason   b. Benjamin Franklin   c. William Billings
    d. John Adams   e. Katherine Lee Bates

3. John Philip Sousa was the composer of
    a. "The Star-Spangled Banner"
    b. "America, the Beautiful"
    c. "Columbia, the Gem of the Ocean"
    d. "Yankee Doodle"
    e. "The Stars and Stripes Forever"

4. American music
    a. was under the shadow of European music until the twentieth century
    b. has been strongly nationalistic since the eighteenth century
    c. makes frequent use of tunes of Native American Indians
    d. has always been mostly popular music
    e. has always had its own separate identity

5. A favorite technique of Charles Ives was
    a. alternating between 6/8 and 3/4 meters
    b. alternating sections between major and minor
    c. incorporating quotations from American songs
    d. writing piano music to be played with only the left hand
    e. asking the players to shuffle their music and then play in the order
       that the pages came out

6. Who was an important composer of ragtime music?
    a. Leonard Bernstein   b. Scott Joplin   c. Duke Ellington
    d. Stephen Foster   e. Louis Armstrong

7. What American city is considered the birthplace of jazz?
    a. New York   b. Chicago   c. New Orleans   d. Los Angeles
    e. Philadelphia

8. A "blue note" in jazz is
   a. any note played with a mute on the instrument
   b. the chords played by the guitar player
   c. a song with a sad text
   d. the lowering of the first, third, or fifth notes of the scale, while leaving the harmony unchanged
   e. a note with a slide or glissando

9. Which are the features of traditional jazz? Mark all that apply.
   a. improvisation
   b. dissonant harmonies
   c. much syncopation
   d. use of mutes on brasses to achieve special effects
   e. slow tempos

10. Who was a famous scat singer?
    a. Bessie Smith   b. Ma Rainey   c. Gloria Estefan   d. Ella Fitzgerald
    e. Bob Dylan

11. The singing style used in country music can be described as
    a. slightly nasal and tense
    b. containing a fast, wide vibrato
    c. deep and warm
    d. somewhat like operatic singing
    e. ornamented often by the singer

12. "Music City USA" refers to
    a. Hollywood   b. New York City   c. New Orleans   d. Nashville   e. Detroit

13. Popular music in America
    a. has developed new and different variants of its styles
    b. has acquired much economic and social importance
    c. is continuously evolving
    d. is as complex as American society itself
    e. All these choices

14. A "hot" style of Latin American music is called
    a. jalapeño   b. hot chili   c. salsa   d. taco taco   e. Cubano

15. Which statements are true about music for films?
    a. movies have almost never been silent
    b. in silent films a pianist played music at appropriate times
    c. a few high quality theaters hired orchestras to play music written for the film
    d. A and B only
    e. A, B, and C only

16. Who is an important composer of film music?
    a. John Williams
    b. George Gershwin
    c. Scott Joplin
    d. Stephen Foster
    e. Leonard Bernstein

Answers to Matching Review Questions

1 – D	11 - M
2 – C	12 - P
3 – B	13 - R
4 – E	14 - T
5 – F	15 - Q
6 - J	16 - N
7 - H	17 - O
8 - G	18 - K
9 - I	19 - S
10 - A	20 - L

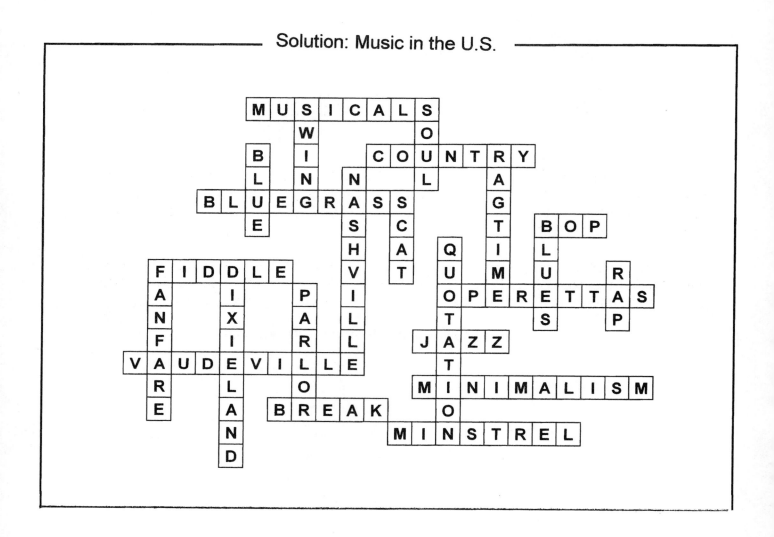

Answers to Multiple Choice Questions

1 – E	6 - B	11 - A	16 - A
2 – C	7 - C	12 - D	
3 – E	8 - D	13 - E	
4 – A	9 - A, C, and D	14 – C	
5 – C	10 - D	15 - E	

PART VIII

Music Around the World

The world is filled with many different kinds of music. Each culture has its own unique music, just as it has its own language and other customs. The music of the people of another culture is just as important and meaningful to them as your favorite type of music is to you.

Knowing something about various types of music that exist around the world is a part of being a citizen of the twenty-first century. Our contacts with people from other places and cultures is continually becoming more frequent and vitally important.

Chapter 40 Review

Folk and Ethnic Music

<u>Main Points</u>

1. Folk music is the music of the common people of a particular nation or ethnic group. Ethnic music is identified with a particular culture, but it may or may not be the music of its common people. Some types of ethnic music are performed by trained musicians.

2. Folk/ethnic music is important to know for three reasons:

- •   Elements of it are often found in concert music
- •   It reveals the attitudes and values of a culture
- •   Today we encounter other cultures more and more

3. Much of the world's music is never written down, even some that has existed for thousands of years. Instead, it is passed from one person or generation to another by word of mouth (oral tradition).

4. Performers of folk music are often expected to improvise. Each type of music has performance traditions and practices that the musicians are expected to follow.

5. Folk/ethnic music differs from concert music because:

- •   It is not uniform or standardized within the culture
- •   The creator of a piece of music is unknown
- •   Individuals feel free to make changes in the music
- •   The performer has a more important role
- •   Much improvisation is expected
- •   An audience, if there is any, is much less important
- •   It contains subtleties that are easily missed by persons from outside that culture
- •   It often exists only by oral tradition
- •   Only in recent decades have serious efforts been made to preserve the various types of folk/ethnic music

6. Cultural elements are more important in folk/ethnic music than they are in concert music. For this reason the cultural background should be kept in mind as much as possible when listening to or studying about folk music.

7. Folk instruments are often divided into four basic groups:

- aerophones -- instruments that are blown by the player
- ideophones -- percussion instruments other than drums
- membranophones -- drums
- chordophones -- instruments that produce sounds from a vibrating string

Musical Terms

folk music
ethnic music
oral tradition
folk instruments
    aerophones
    ideophones
    membranophones
    chordophones

Chapter 41 Review

Folk Music of Europe and the Americas

Main Points

1. European folk music is similar to our Western music in many respects, such as in the use of major and minor harmony and metrical rhythm. But many folk melodies use seven-note scales other than major or minor, called modes. A pentatonic scale has five notes arranged in the pattern of the black keys of the piano.

2. Many European folk songs are strophic, with different verses or words sung to the same melody. Many are ballads in which the singer relates a story, often a sad one, in five or more verses. One of the most famous ballads is "Barbara Allen."

3. American folk music is a combination of music from many different sources, especially the British Isles. Broadsides (songs with the words printed on a single sheet of paper) were early popular examples. The name comes from the old English practice of printing ballads on large sheets of paper called broadsides, which were sold on the streets.

4. There are several types of American folk music, including work songs, occupational songs, dance music, and songs that allow the singer to express his or her feelings. Some folk songs have been arranged for public concert performance.

5. Dance music was often played on fiddles. Square dancing was the most important type of folk dancing, and the tunes, called hoedowns or breakdowns, were in a fast tempo in duple meter.

6. Native American music varied considerable according to the tribe and region. Most of it is functional music. It has not had a noticeable impact on American music; most Native Americans have lived apart on reservations, and Native American music is too different from Western music to be easily assimilated.

7. Many features of African American music have been incorporated into American music. Types of African American music include the spontaneous calls and hollers heard in the fields, spirituals, work songs, and folk blues, which were songs for individual singers to cry out against life's problems.

8. Latin American music is a combination from a variety of sources – especially Spanish, Indian, and African.

9. Mexican music is more Spanish in character than many types of Latin American music. Mexicans developed a ballad-type song called a corrido or son, and also have many mariachi bands. These popular bands consist of from three to twelve musicians who walk around playing violins, guitars, trumpets, and other instruments.

Musical Terms

modes   spiritual
pentatonic   mariachi band
ballad   call and holler
strophic   folk blues
broadside   corrido; son
hoedown
fiddle

Chapter 42 Review

Music of Africa and the Middle East

Main Points

1. African music is:

- strongly related to the language being sung
- often associated with dancing
- rhythmically complex
- improvised according to its stylistic guidelines
- functional music
- often quite different from one tribe to another

2. You will frequently hear call-and-response patterns in African music in which the leader sings or plays a phrase then the group responds. The melodies are often altered and ornamented (with decorative notes, slides, trills, changes of pitch, and so forth).

3. Africans have animistic beliefs about musical instruments; the instruments take on an almost human quality. "Talking drums" attempt to imitate the pitches and inflections of the language and can be understood by the people who speak that language.

4. Middle Eastern music is complex and based on often conflicting theories that are loosely followed. A few restrained prayers and chants are performed in a singsong style in the mosque, but they are not officially considered music.

5. Many ornaments are added to melodies by singers of Middle Eastern music, and several instruments are characteristic of the region: the ud, rebab, and tombak.

6. The music of Israel is very cosmopolitan, except for its religious music. But Judaic music varies according to the degree of orthodoxy of a particular congregation.

Musical Terms

call-and-response
ornaments; ornamentation

Chapter 43 Review

Music of Asia

Main Points

1. Melodies in Indian classical music are developed around ragas, which are melodic formulas believed to express feelings. Rhythm in Indian music is based on talas, which are rhythmic cycles usually from five to eight counts in length.

2. Instruments associated with Indian classical music include the sitar (a string instrument), pungi (a wind instrument), and tabla (a percussion instrument). Concerts are very informal. There is no printed program; the performance is not planned out and the performers don't play from notation. Conversing with each other or with the audience is acceptable.

3. Indian music is bound up in the religious culture. Indian musicians believe music is the mystical transfer of human emotion into sound, or *bhava*.

4. Chinese music is based on the five-note pentatonic scale and features certain instruments such as the pipa, erhu, flutes, and percussion.

5. Japanese music features a large string instrument called the koto. Other instruments include a type of flute and a small string instrument called the shamisen. The music uses the five-note pentatonic scale and is refined and subtle.

6. The island of Bali in the country of Indonesia is famous for its gamelan (instrumental ensembles) and dance. Gamelan contain drums, flute, and especially the kajar, which looks like a small metal pot with a knobbed lid. Balinese music also uses the five-note pentatonic scale, complex rhythmic patterns, and colorful timbres. Cymbals, gongs, and xylophone-like instruments contribute to the gentle sounds.

Musical Terms

raga
tala
gamelan
pentatonic

NOTABLE FEATURES OF FOLK-ETHNIC MUSIC

- The original creators are rarely known
- Improvisation is very important
- Almost all types of folk/ethnic music contain many subtleties
- Often preserved by oral tradition
- Cultural aspects are extremely important in understanding the music
- Folk instruments are divided into four classifications: aerophones, ideophones, membranophones, and chordophones
- Pentatonic scales and modes are often used
- The ballad is important in English and American folk music
- African American influence is important to American music
- Latin American music is a mixture of Spanish, Indian, and African influences
- African music features complex rhythmic structures and call-and-response patterns
- Classical Indian music uses ragas and talas and singing accompanied by the sitar
- Balinese music features instrumental ensembles called gamelan

---

Discussion and Critical Thinking

1. Should an effort be made to preserve our traditional folk music? Or is commercial popular music the folk music of today?

2. Are you familiar with any types of folk/ethnic music presented in the text? Why does some of this music sound so different to many of us?

3. How can you locate performances of folk/ethnic music in your area?

Part VIII Review Questions

These questions are a review of information and terminology using three different formats: matching, crossword puzzle, and multiple choice. The answers are found on pages 174-175.

Matching. Match each term with its correct definition by placing the appropriate letter in the space provided.

_____ 1. Spiritual   _____ 6. Ornamentation

_____ 2. Pentatonic   _____ 7. Folk Blues

_____ 3. Strophic   _____ 8. Call-and-Response

_____ 4. Improvisation   _____ 9. Oral tradition

_____ 5. Folk Music   _____ 10. Ballad

DEFINITIONS

A.   A song in which several verses of words are sung to the same melody
B.   An English narrative song told in simple verses
C.   The process by which music is preserved by people hearing it, remembering it, then performing it
D.   Music of the common people of a society or geographical area
E.   The most important type of secular folk music among African Americans
F.   Music that is made up on the spot, usually according to stylistic guidelines
G.   Form found in African music in which phrases of music are exchanged between leader and group
H.   Five-note scale pattern similar to the arrangement of whole and half steps on the black keys of the piano
I.   A form of African American religious folk music sung by a group
J.   Melodic decoration and embellishment either improvised or indicated by signs in the music

Music Around the World

ACROSS

2 song in which several verses of words are sung to the same melody
4 English narrative song told in simple verses
8 type of tradition in which music is preserved by people hearing and performing it
10 music that is made up on the spot
12 bands that perform throughout Mexico
14 five-note scale pattern
15 most important type of secular folk music among African Americans
16 violin adapted for country music
18 portion of a square dance

DOWN

1 rhythmic cycle of beats found in the music of India
3 melodic decoration and embellishment
5 form of African American religious folk music sung by a group
6 music of the common people of a society or geographical area
7 Mexican ballad-like song
9 melodic formula used in the music of India
11 Balinese instrumental ensemble
12 scale patterns containing seven pitches other than major or minor
13 form of African music in which phrases of music are exchanged first as a call and then as this
17 music that is characteristic of a particular culture or group

Multiple Choice. Circle the correct answer.

1. Which statements are <u>true</u> about folk/ethnic music?
    a. All folk music is also ethnic music.
    b. All ethnic music is also folk music.
    c. Folk music is the music of the common people of a nation or ethnic group.
    d. Ethnic music represents its culture but not the music of the common people of that culture.
    e. Ethnic music represents the efforts of an elite group of musicians.

2. Which is a characteristic of folk/ethnic music?
    a. the composer of the song is known
    b. the performer is expected to perform the song accurately
    c. the reaction of the audience is very important to the performer
    d. most folks songs around the world sound quite a bit alike
    e. much of the music is improvised

3. Oral tradition
    a. applies only to vocal music
    b. is the retaining of music from simply listening to it
    c. consists of verbal descriptions of a type of folk music
    d. is the preservation of a song in its original language
    e. is the practice of singing a song from looking at written instructions

4. Which statement is <u>not</u> true about music and culture?
    a. All music is a product of a particular culture.
    b. Music and the other arts present insight into a society's character.
    c. It is not necessary to know the culture of a people to really know and understand their music.
    d. Works of Western art music are more able to stand alone without reference to everyday cultural that most folk/ethnic types of music.
    e. Until the twentieth century scholars did not seem to care much about folk/ethnic music.

5. A strophic song is one that
    a. is sung by one singer accompanied by a guitar or similar instrument
    b. is sung by a small group of singers
    c. has several sets of words sung to the same melody
    d. has all its words set to different music
    e. is sung without accompaniment

6. The most common form of the blues is
    a. *aba*   b. *abb*   c. *aab*   d. *abab*   e. *abc*

7. A feature of rhythm in African music is
    a. polyrhythms
    b. two-beat meter
    c. three-beat meter
    d. free rhythm

8. The African instrument the mbria is a
    a. drum with an hourglass shape
    b. thumb piano
    c. rattle
    d. set of two drums each with a different pitch
    e. a large drum played with a stick

9. A raga is a
    a. rhythm pattern in Balinese music
    b. rhythm pattern in Indian music
    c. melodic formula in Balinese music
    d. melodic formula in Indian music
    e. type of string instrument used in Indian classical music

10. Which instrument is associated with Japanese music?
    a. koto   b. sitar   c. ud   d. tombak   e. pipa

11. Chordophones are folk instruments that
    a. sound chords
    b. involve the player blowing air into them
    c. produce sounds when struck by the hand or a stick
    d. produce sounds on a string
    e. are only used for accompanying singers

Answers to Matching Review Questions

1 – I	6 – J
2 – H	7 – E
3 – A	8 – G
4 – F	9 – C
5 – D	10 – B

Flashcards of Music Terminolgy

The following pages can be cut apart and made into flashcards for your use. Each music term has a brief definition on the reverse side. The part of the book in which the term appears is indicated on the front side, as well as the chapter in which the term is discussed or first presented.

We hope that these flashcards will be useful to you in learning some of the important musical concepts and information.